CHANGING THE
POWERS THAT BE

CHANGING THE
POWERS THAT BE

How the Left Can Stop Losing and Win

G. William Domhoff

ROWMAN & LITTLEFIELD PUBLISHERS, INC.
Lanham • Boulder • New York • Oxford

ROWMAN & LITTLEFIELD PUBLISHERS, INC.

Published in the United States of America
by Rowman & Littlefield Publishers, Inc.
A Member of the Rowman & Littlefield Publishing Group
4501 Forbes Boulevard, Suite 200, Lanham, Maryland 20706
www.rowmanlittlefield.com

P.O. Box 317, Oxford OX2 9RU, United Kingdom

British Library Cataloguing in Publication Information Available

Library of Congress Cataloging-in-Publication Data

Domhoff, G. William.
 Changing the powers that be : how the Left can stop losing and win /
G. William Domhoff.
   p. cm.
 Includes bibliographical references and index.
 ISBN 0-7425-2491-4 (cloth : alk. paper)
  1. Liberalism—United States 2. Political campaigns—United States
 3. United States—Politics and government—2001– I. Title.
JC574.2 .U6 D66 2003
320.51'3'0973—dc21

                                                        2002015714

Printed in the United States of America

⊗ ™ The paper used in this publication meets the minimum requirements
of American National Standard for Information Sciences—Permanence of
Paper for Printed Library Materials, ANSI/NISO Z39.48-1992.

CONTENTS

Preface   vii

1 The What-If Nader Campaign of 2000   1

2 Why Egalitarians Should Transform the Democratic Party   17

3 More Equality through the Market System   39

4 Social Movements and Strategic Nonviolence   49

5 Redefining Who's Us and Who's Them   63

6 Keeping Leaders Accountable   71

7 A New Foreign Policy and a New Stance on Religion   85

8 Stop Blaming the Media   99

9 Making the Future Yours   105

Annotated Bibliography and Source Notes   109

Acknowledgments   131

Index   133

About the Author   143

PREFACE

It isn't hard to figure out if you want to read this book. Just breeze through the first three or four paragraphs of any chapter. Or read the last paragraph of the last chapter and work backwards from there. Either way would give you the flavor of the book.

Wherever you start, it should make sense right away and it should sound like we are having a conversation. There is much to ponder, some of it decidedly against the grain, but the book is meant to be a smooth read. No footnotes, no long passages borrowed from other books, no name-dropping. The citations and suggested further readings are all saved for the end in the "Annotated Bibliography and Source Notes" section.

Changing the Powers That Be is about how there could be greater equality, fairness, and opportunity for everyone. It's about positive social changes that would make the United States a better place, and a better world citizen. It shows that these goals are attainable if the right strategies are combined into a dynamic new package and several losing strategies are abandoned.

It assumes that most Americans have believed since the founding of the country that there should be equality, fairness, and opportunity for everyone who lives here. It says that American activists have achieved many of their goals through a wide variety of social and political movements, everything from the New Deal to the civil rights, feminist, environmental, living wage, and anti-sweatshop movements.

It claims that average Americans have won these advances against great odds—the economic and political systems mostly operate in favor of the powers that be, giving in to the pressures and rationalizations of the wealthy few and their corporations. Since 1980, these tendencies in favor of the rich and powerful have gotten completely out of hand, generating excesses that haven't been seen since the fabled Gilded Age of the 1890s.

The country has moved very far from its people-first and cooperative values. It is grinding down and discouraging the great majority of people through low wages, long working hours, job insecurity, poor health care programs, and inadequate schools. A small percentage of people are doing very well, but most are just struggling to stay even, or keep from going under.

And yet, this book says that new opportunities to create positive social changes are arising all the time. There are always new openings where new ideas could be applied. The cracks and fissures in the powers that be were exploited in the past and could be exploited again.

This book presents a whole new approach to how Americans could achieve more of their long-sought goals. It explains why the old approaches to positive social change have failed badly. It even dares to suggest that the most prominent critics of government policy are off base. Their ideas are proven failures. They have become part of the problem. They had their chance, and they mostly blew it. For those who want greater equality, fairness, and opportunity, it is time for a fresh start.

In chapter 1 you can see what should have happened in the presidential elections of 2000. Chapter 3 explains how greater energy independence, better health benefits, and more economic equality could be realized while maintaining freedom and opportunity. In chapter 5 you can find a new way to figure out who's us and who's them. Chapter 7 presents a new stance on foreign policy that emphasizes support for human rights, religious freedom, and democratic governments everywhere. Or, if you like, you can start with the short last chapter on "Making the Future Yours." It's that kind of book.

1

THE WHAT-IF NADER CAMPAIGN OF 2000

Imagine the following plausible scenario: Ralph Nader's decision to challenge Albert Gore Jr. in the Democratic presidential primaries in 2000 will go down in history as a major turning point for Americans who seek greater equality, fairness, and opportunity for everyone in all areas of life from the personal to the economic to the political. It begins the transformation of the Democratic Party and maybe of the United States as well. It already has triggered several positive consequences by energizing egalitarian activists inside and outside the electoral arena, putting the forces of reaction on the defensive for the first time in many years.

Not that it was an easy decision for Nader to go Democrat. He needed a lot of convincing and almost went along with those who urged that he run as a third-party candidate because of the timidity and caution of many present-day Democrats. In the end, however, Nader was persuaded by comparative political studies of two dozen countries. They show it is rare for a third party to develop in countries that have an electoral system like the one in America—called a "single-member district plurality system"—where it only takes the most votes to win, not a majority, and where candidates run for seats from specific geographical districts, like a House district. It's a system that creates a powerful pressure to create preelection coalitions with the people closest to you in viewpoint. Otherwise, the party you least prefer may end up winning even though less than a majority favors it.

This electoral system makes a party of the left or right a mortal threat to the two large coalitional parties that build out from right of center and left of center. Even 1 or 2 percent of the vote can make all the difference in the world if the loser ends up with, say, 48 percent of the vote and would have won with 50.1 percent if he or she had been able to capture the third-party votes. Thus, the basic problem for egalitarians: a vote for a third party of the left is a vote for the Republicans because it allows them to win even if they don't have the support of the majority. Even worse, a vote for a third party of the left ignores the short-run concerns of the average citizens who believe that their lives are at least a little better on one or another seemingly small issue when the Democrats are in power.

So Democrat voters end up disliking those who voted for a third party of the left, and the liberals and egalitarians are at each others' throats right from the start. This is the first and basic dilemma confronting those who seek greater equality, fairness, and opportunity for everyone. They are divided among themselves in facing a corporate-financed Republican opposition that to begin with is already very powerful. Until this dilemma is resolved, there is no hope whatsoever of creating a majority for progressive social change.

Now, there are a few countries with this kind of system where there is a third party, but it is usually one that represents a specific region or ethnic group. These little third parties can have an impact when they choose which major party to join with to form a parliamentary majority, but such postelectoral coalitions are not to be in the United States because it has a presidential, not a parliamentary, system. Single-member plurality districts and a strong presidency, itself rooted in one giant single-member district called the United States, dictate that coalitions must be formed before the election by people who want to avoid being governed by their least-favored party. Hence the two preelectoral coalitions called the Democratic and Republican Parties, which have been dominated by rival factions of the ownership class since the 1790s.

Imagine, too, that Nader not only grasped this deadly structural logic, but that he learned from the disastrous history of previous leftist third parties, especially the Progressive Party of 1948. The formation of that party led to bitter battles between "liberals," who stayed with the Democrats, and "progressives" (mostly communists, socialists, and pacifists), who backed former vice president Henry Wallace as the third-party candidate. Despite Wallace's strong reputation among liberals and his high name recognition in the electorate, thanks to several important government positions he held from 1933 to 1946, he received only a little more than one million votes. Worse, his campaign set in motion the events that finished off the strong left-liberal-labor coalition within the Democratic Party that slowly developed during the New Deal years. Nader also knew that the Peace and Freedom Party of 1968 and the Citizen's Party of 1980 had zero positive impact.

Nader further understood that the two major political parties are now in part an extension of the government. First, the government "registers" citizens as "members" of one or another party, which means the party cannot even control its own membership by refusing admittance or expelling dissidents. Second, the government conducts "primaries" in which any member of the party can run on any platform he or she so desires, thereby contending with big money donors and their hired experts for control of the party. From a governmental perspective, the "Democratic Party" is merely the name for one of the two structured pathways into government. It's now a shell, which is a long way from the days when court house gangs controlled nominations in the South and city bosses decided on candidates in most big cities in the North.

Nor was it lost on Nader that insurgencies in party primaries have done much better than third-party candidates over the past seventy years. The most famous example is socialist Upton Sinclair's switch to the Democrats in 1934 so he could run for governor in the California party's primary, where he won 51 percent of the vote in a field of seven candidates, and went on to take 37 percent of the vote in the regular election against the incumbent Republican. The success of the New Right in transforming the Republican Party by running candidates in the primaries was not overlooked by Nader either. So the combination of structure and history came down in favor of a Democratic insurgency. Third-party advocates were displeased, but not the great majority of Nader admirers and those leftists who suffered through the lean times of the last thirty-plus years.

Not that there was a groundswell of voters for Nader at first, or even later. It looked for months like he was going nowhere; established political operatives and the media focused on Gore and Bill Bradley. But when Bradley dropped out and Nader refused to quit, things began to get interesting. Suddenly, there was more media attention because it was a David and Goliath story at a time when there was not much other news. Moreover, Nader's principled decision to avoid personal attacks on Gore, along with his laser focus on the tremendous failures of big corporations, and his equal emphasis on the great possibilities of using government to tame them, gained him increasing respect. Nader's slogan was also ideal for showing that there are more egalitarian Democrats than the centrists like to think: "Send Gore a message about social equality and the importance of the environment."

Nader was wildly outspent, of course, by more than twenty to one, due to Gore's many connections to big corporations and their lobbyists. This disadvantage naturally made it tough for him to give Gore a full challenge, but he knew that he would have had the same problem running as a third-party candidate in the regular elections. He also knew that campaign finance can be overrated if a candidate has name recognition and a strong message. He therefore concentrated initially on meetings with small groups so he could build a solid core who would spread the word gradually through friendship networks. Interviews with a few friendly journalists also got the word out, along with low-cost ads in local newspapers in the cities he was visiting.

It was the huge rallies at arena after arena across the country that really ignited the campaign. Thousands of people turned out in small cities up and down the Left Coast, along with nearly ten thousand in Chicago and Washington, and fifteen thousand at Madison Square Garden. Student audiences in Boston and other college towns were ecstatic for Nader. It was just like what the old days of grassroots politics were imagined to be, and even the skeptical and disaffected began to enjoy the campaign. They also admired the dogged way in which Nader insisted on visiting every state and speaking in every venue, even ones unlikely to give him any votes. Then a few clever and humorous television ads in a handful of relatively inexpensive markets added to the excitement and fun as Gore soldiered on in his usual stolid way.

Still, Nader never won more than 20 to 25 percent of the votes in any primary, even in California and Oregon. But he never got less than 5 to 10 percent either, whereas he would have been lucky to take 3 percent as a third-party candidate in the regular elections. Overall, his vote totals were far more than the Gore campaign expected, forcing Gore to respect the egalitarian wing of the party, but less than Nader hoped for, a sobering reminder to insurgents that they have their work cut out for them if they expect to attract the many people they think of as their "natural" allies.

But Nader's overall showing was enough to make it necessary for Gore to allow him to speak at the convention. The negotiations were intense, with Gore's handlers trying to keep Nader's appearance short and far from prime time, but ten minutes in the early evening wasn't bad, and the speech was a bell ringer that is available on video to rally new activists for years to come. Rehearsing once again the many failures and injustices of a raw antigovernment capitalism that doesn't worry about health care needs or clean air or poverty, and explaining the many remedies available by government planning through the market system, Nader then cemented his future role by praising Gore and calling for his election. Saying those positive words wasn't easy for him, because he felt that Gore had treated him and other egalitarian activists shabbily over the previous eight years, but there was just enough politician in him to squeeze the words out.

Gore, of course, did not return the favor, saying little or nothing about Nader during the regular campaign, and limiting his official role to a few fringe appearances. Not that Nader was a wilting lily; as a supporter of the party's candidate, he took advantage of the campaign fervor to visit liberals and egalitarians on his own hook everywhere he could, working to convince the few remaining holdouts for futile third parties that they could have more influence inside the Democratic Party than outside it. He also used these visits to start egalitarian Democratic clubs (EDCs) in forty-three states, laying the basis for the future takeover of the party in the same way liberals had taken over the California state party with their California democratic clubs in the 1950s. He also used these occasions to make plans for the national postelection EDC convention that was held in March 2001, where club members were given the task of developing a more detailed set of programs for future elections and urged to find candidates to carry the egalitarian message in state and congressional races.

Although Gore continued to ignore Nader after his narrow victory, which was decided late in the evening by the electoral votes in New Hampshire and Florida, he quietly paid off the left with several of his second- and third-level appointments. Former Naderites gained some influence at the Environmental Protection Agency and Occupational Safety and Health Administration, where they implemented several rulings and regulations that the Clinton-Gore team had been sitting on because they did not want to stir up the corporate pressure groups.

Nader's decision to help send a moderate Democrat to the White House also made good sense in terms of the leverage it gave liberal Democrats in the Senate, such as Jon Corzine, the new senator from New Jersey. Chastised by purists for spending tens of millions of his own money to win the seat, the former Wall Street investment banker is nonetheless the most progressive Democratic senator with real leadership potential and a grasp of the inner workings of capitalism to appear in two decades. Moreover, Nader earned credit for helping the Democrats come very close to a House majority, thanks to last-minute victories in districts in Michigan, New

Jersey, and New Mexico, where his visits helped to reduce the vote for Green Party candidates just enough for the Democrats to squeak by.

Nader's tireless work within the Democratic Party helped to close the already narrowing gap between "liberals" and "progressives-socialists-radicals," a process that has been underway for many years for a variety of reasons. But it was not just his tireless work. Nader also forcefully articulated the point now brilliantly demonstrated by several outstanding economists—it is possible to modify the worst aspects of capitalism to a considerable degree through market-based planning based on taxes, subsidies, government purchases, and regulations. There is no such thing as a "free market" that can operate without careful government regulation, as demonstrated once again by the scam artists from Enron, Global Crossing, and other fraudulent "new economy" companies, not to mention all the slick hustlers on Wall Street, but the centralized, nonmarket planning that is the essence of "socialism" doesn't work either. So the issue is not planning, as Nader patiently explained, but what kind of government planning and by whom, which means the basic necessity is political power within a market system.

Although Nader was unrelenting in his criticism of corporations and those individuals and groups who support the economic and political status quo, he was careful not to attack "the capitalists," "the rich," or "the ruling class." That's because he didn't buy into the overly simple assumption that everyone currently in those categories is an inevitable opponent of egalitarian social change. Even though there is a dominant social class of corporate owners and top executives, who have different interests from people who work for wages and salaries, it did not make sense to him to rely on a class-based "us" versus "them" framing. He understood that the issue is ultimately a value-based program and political power, and he knew from past experience that some members of the ownership class might come to support part or all of his platform. In fact, knowing that defectors from an elite group can be very important to insurgent causes, he emphasized that many wealthy people already were among his supporters. He therefore confined himself to attacks on corporate greed and those who oppose greater equality, fairness, and opportunity. He defined the opposition as the "corporate-conservative coalition" and the Republican Party. In so doing he drew on the magnificent example of the early civil rights movement, which wisely refused to label all whites as enemies, but only racists and bigots, and thereby provided an opening whereby prejudiced whites could change their minds and adopt new values in the light of new information and changing circumstances.

In addition, Nader's long-standing connections with grassroots social movement organizations means that the EDCs will be able to call on these organizations to generate the pressure on elected officials that has to be exerted on every issue that comes up for a vote, either to be sure these officials don't collapse to the center, or to give them cover for what they want to do anyhow. By being inside and outside of electoral politics, the wider egalitarian movement he is championing can have the best of both worlds. Most of the time its members can continue to work in specific environmental, social justice, or workplace organizations that have no electoral focus, but they also can involve themselves periodically in electoral politics through the EDCs.

Moreover, Nader put a strong emphasis on the power of what is now called "strategic nonviolence," or nonviolent direct action, stressing that is the only method for prevailing in a conflict that is consistent with maintaining and expanding political democracy. He and his forces thereby tried to marginalize those activists whose calls for property destruction and retaliatory attacks on the police at demonstrations have undermined the outreach potential of the global justice movement. In focusing on nonviolence, Nader urged that activists now build on the work of the strategists who have catalogued many dozens of nonviolent direct-action tactics and documented their usefulness in a variety of countries and settings. In particular, they can draw inspiration and training methods from the early civil rights movement, which was a picture-perfect example of the power of strategic nonviolence through its combination of sit-ins, freedom rides, boycotts, and marches.

No matter what the future may bring in the face of a formidable corporate power structure and a great many citizens satisfied with the status quo, Nader's decision to take egalitarian activism into the Democratic Party was a sensational expenditure of moral capital, providing egalitarians with new hope and a new direction.

✳   ✳   ✳

Well, that's the way it should have been. If that scenario had been carried out, the United States would look very different today, and those seeking greater equality, fairness, and opportunity would be making plans to expand on their successes. Why, then, do so many egalitarians try to build new third parties of the left in the face of overwhelming structural odds and terrible historical precedents, always ending up with a meager few percent of the vote, far less than they expect? Then, too, why is there no sustained effort to create programs for greater fairness and equality based on planning through the market, a decentralized approach consistent with democratic participation in the political arena? Furthermore, why are so many egalitarians hesitant to speak out against violent tactics at demonstrations, thereby implicitly conceding moral leadership to those who think that the destruction of property or violence toward persons are a virtue or an eventual necessity? For that matter, why do many egalitarian groups end up with unresponsive leaders, embrace foreign revolutions that end up with undemocratic regimes, or sometimes engage in unnecessary conflict with organized religion?

If you have ever asked yourself any of these questions, then this book is meant for you. It should be of interest to all those trying to learn more about large-scale social change, as well as to more detached bystanders who wonder why egalitarians so often fail even though they have the best of intentions and the great energy that comes from strong moral conviction. To give the analysis more punch, however, it is written as if it were explicitly addressed to those potential activists who are not satisfied with the answers provided by any of the egalitarian activists currently on the scene, whether they try to realize their goals as progressives, Greens, socialists, revolutionary Marxists, or anarchists. It is also addressed to those experienced activists who have come to doubt the usefulness of much of what they have been doing. But it most likely will not be enjoyed by those already committed to one or another leftist party or project, who probably will read it with increasing dismay.

Think of this book as a report from a consultant whose advice can be used or discarded as you see fit. I present what I have to say in this way because being a consultant is a comfortable role for me and reduces any potential tension in our relationship. I also believe I can be more frank as a consultant. I feel like I can say things that may upset current activists without them immediately closing the book. This approach also makes it easier for me to be highly critical of claims put forth by the respected theorists that most egalitarians seem to draw on. Being a consultant also makes it clear that I make no pretense to any activist credentials.

My stance as a consultant also allows me to comment more candidly about some key ideas in Marxism that continue to have an influence in some leftist groups. Criticism of any aspect of Marxism is second only to third parties as a source of great emotion and division among leftists. Moreover, many new activists may wonder if there is any relevance to discussing Marxist ideas, which they see as a leftover from a failed past. But key mistakes related to central planning, markets, and foreign policy need to be discussed briefly so that new activists can make sure they do not repeat them. The prominent activists who continue to advocate these ideas are small in number, but they have had a large indirect impact on many egalitarian movements because many parts of their analysis are accepted as starting points.

My advice as a consultant is based on my analysis of the American power structure. Briefly put, it is my conclusion that the United States is increasingly dominated by a corporate-conservative coalition that is rooted in the ownership and control of large corporations, banks, and agribusinesses, which are closely coordinated by shared directors, corporate lawyers, and management consultants even while they compete for profits in the marketplace. This corporate-conservative coalition dominates general government policymaking through a policy-planning network based in foundations, think tanks, and policy-discussion groups. It thereby maintains a near-monopoly of respectable expert opinion, which ranges from the mildly liberal to the highly conservative, and never questions the fact that the top 1 percent now own almost half of all marketable assets. This corporate-based coalition also employs a vast armada of lobbyists who further the narrow and short-range interests of specific corporations and wealthy families by finding them tax breaks, subsidies, and loopholes in government regulations. The corporate-conservative coalition now operates primarily through the Republican Party in the political arena, although it also maintains a strong presence in the presidential wing of the Democratic Party through large campaign donations to its favored candidates.

None of this means the corporate-conservative coalition has complete and total power, or that its success in each new policy conflict is a foregone conclusion. For example, lawyers and other highly trained professionals with an interest in consumer or environmental issues are able to use lawsuits to win governmental restrictions on some corporate practices and even to challenge whole industries. Wage and salary workers, when they are organized into unions and have the right to strike, can gain pay increases and social benefits such as health insurance. In addition, the several opponents of the corporate-conservatives, such as civil rights organizations, locally based environmental organizations, liberal trade union leaders, liberal churches, and liberal university communities, sometimes work together on policy issues within the Democratic Party as a "liberal-labor coalition."

However, the liberal-labor coalition seldom wins more than a few minor concessions and is extremely difficult to hold together because its members have divergent and sometimes clashing interests, which leads some of them to side with the Republicans on a few issues. It has far less money to spend on political campaigns than the corporate-conservatives. It also has great difficulty assembling a political majority within the electorate because of the long-standing racial and religious divisions that continue to matter deeply in American life. For all these reasons, freedom of speech, freedom of assembly, and the right to organized and vote matter much less than they otherwise would.

Because I am a power analyst, the general argument in this book hinges on the power dimension in human societies, whether at the interpersonal, group, or societal level. Power is only one of several dimensions in the human experience, along with love, cooperation, esthetics, intellectual curiosity, and many more, but it is the dimension that plays the central role in all the problems that are of concern in this book. It's the dimension that leads to bullies, rival gangs, enforced cooperation, hierarchy, ruling elites, and ruling classes. For my purposes here, power is best thought of as running along an egalitarian-domination dimension that shapes all human interactions and social structures, with egalitarians at one end and dominators at the other. Egalitarians are those who want to minimize arbitrary authority and hierarchy, and who believe that everyone should be accorded the same opportunity and respect in the political, economic, legal, and personal realms of life. They deny that some individuals or groups are better than others, although they recognize that some individuals, but not groups, have unusual gifts for activities like art, athletics, music, or scientific research. Dominators, on the other hand, think that there are inherent inequalities among individuals and groups that justifiably lead to extreme hierarchy and social stratification. Down through the centuries they have believed in male superiority, racial superiority, and the need for kingships and nobilities to control ordinary people. In the nineteenth century, they wanted to restrict the vote to property owners, and now they believe that Euro-Americans work harder and have better moral character than most other people.

The egalitarian-domination dimension in human affairs has much overlap with the liberal-conservative dimension in American politics, a dimension that has been shown to almost perfectly differentiate members of

Congress by their voting records since the 1790s. (The only separate dimension that adds any new information concerns attitudes toward racial equality.) By and large, liberals have been for all the progressive changes that are now taken for granted, even by conservatives. The conservatives generally opposed all these changes. In recent times, for example, they resisted feminism, racial integration, and the extension of civil liberties and democratic rights.

But I speak of an egalitarian-domination dimension, not a liberal-conservative one, because it better captures the values and energy of those inside and outside of electoral politics who have been the force for liberal and progressive changes. Egalitarians are the people who have been feminists, union organizers, socialists, communists, strong environmentalists, civil rights activists, and gay and lesbian activists as well as elected liberals. Egalitarianism is the underlying value system that animates all of them, even though they differ greatly among themselves in the policies and strategies they embrace in order to realize their values. In particular, egalitarians have often clashed with liberals (now called "reformers" by those egalitarians who self-identity as "radicals") even though both camps are on the same side of the fence. Understanding this clash and helping to overcome it is one of the goals of this book.

This positive characterization of egalitarianism does not mean that egalitarians themselves always have practiced what they preach. The elitist thinking that characterizes dominators can be a subtle and insidious foe, and it is especially seductive to leaders as they become more honored, powerful, and self-important. Egalitarians can fall into various elitist traps that are discussed throughout the book, including domination by behind-the-scenes leaders in seemingly leaderless communal or affinity groups. They can become so morally disgusted that they withdraw as much as they can from the activities of everyday life or come to believe that they know what is best for others because of their high moral purpose. To avoid these tendencies, this book suggests that they should define themselves as catalysts and organizers who renounce the possibility of any power for themselves in the world they want to create. Then they can feel free to express their justifiable moral outrage over inequality and injustice without any fear that it might carry them down unproductive pathways. To become trusted and respected through their words and deeds, they have to devise strategies that make it impossible for them to end up as dominators.

Even if elitist thinking and domineering action are overcome, there may also be sociological limits to the degree of organizational equality that can be achieved in a huge industrialized society. There can be considerably greater equality in terms of opportunity and access within the economic and political realms, and greater personal freedom such as has been fought for and won since the 1960s, one of the genuine achievements of the many civil rights, feminist, and gay and lesbian organizations that participate in the liberal-labor coalition. But organizations need leadership, which means that in this domain the emphasis may have to be on leaders being account- able and replaceable.

In addition, it must be stressed that the egalitarian-domination dimen- sion is not one of "good folks" versus "bad folks" when it comes to violence or personality types. Generally speaking, egalitarians have been as prone to use violence as other human beings. Furthermore, individual egalitarians are as likely to be difficult, egotistical, or obnoxious as members of any other group. The pleasant-unpleasant dimension seems to be independent of the egalitarian-domination dimension.

What this book does is to suggest viable pathways to realizing egalitarian values in twenty-first-century America by evaluating what egalitarians have done in the past one hundred years as socialists, progressives, and other kinds of activists. It shows that criticizing one or another of these egalitarian projects, such as, say, socialism, is not the same thing as rejecting the underlying egalitarian ethos. The book does not claim to have all the answers, and it does not try to formulate specific policies or programs, but it does ask the right questions about how to proceed, and it does have many plausible answers based on a wide range of sources and experiences. It is clear on what hasn't worked and won't work, and it suggests that it is time to try something different. It covers what I see as the full range of chal- lenges facing egalitarian activists in the United States. Its contribution, if any, lies in the atypical combination of strategies that it endorses, along with its call for abandoning proven failures that waste needed energy—like start- ing a third party.

To emphasize the need for a fresh start based on enduring values, the book adopts the term "egalitarians" to describe the wide range of current- day activists. It does so first of all because there is a need for a term that encompasses the commonalities of the activists in different areas, who tend to see themselves as separate and distinctive from one another. Even more, the new term is needed because the old designations, such as "progressive" and "socialist," have accumulated too many meanings, most of them nega- tive. They call forth memories of the past, and they remind activists of the disagreements among them. It is time to adopt a new characterization for

a new beginning, and "egalitarians" is a good candidate. It has positive con-
notations for nearly everyone and perfectly characterizes left activists and
what they are seeking, referring as it does to people who advocate the doc-
trine of equal political, economic, and legal rights for all citizens.

Although the book is often critical of past strategies, it does not say
everything egalitarians do is counterproductive. To the contrary, egalitarians played a catalytic role in every movement that led to the expansion of
individual rights and opportunities in the United States in the twentieth
century, starting with the women's suffrage campaign, the creation of
industrial unions, and the civil rights movement, and continuing today in
movements for gender equality, racial and ethnic equality, environmental
protection, and rights for gays and lesbians. In each case, new nonviolent
methods have been invented by egalitarians to disrupt the routines and
belief systems of those who favor the status quo, everything from strikes to
sit-ins to outing to locking down.

So, too, the living-wage and antisweatshop campaigns have been brilliantly done. They have made just the right use of research, litigation, strategic nonviolence, and media. They also serve as a very useful model
because they raise all the right issues about the limits of markets and
because they provide links among so many different groups, such as immigrant workers in the United States, college students who have leverage on
their home campuses, urban activists calling for a living wage, trade unions
with lobbying connections to local and state government, and low-income
workers in less developed countries. Their efforts can be built on and have
the potential to contribute to a larger egalitarian movement, but they are
also a good model because they can succeed on their own terms even if
they do not trigger a more general movement. No self-styled consultant
could improve on them as a superb use of limited resources and as a way
to inspire new activists of an egalitarian stripe.

Even if the overall program suggested in this book were carried out to
the letter, however, there can be no guarantee that it would be a sure thing.
Big corporations have enormous resources, plenty of friends in both political parties, and the loyalty of tens of millions of citizens who believe that
American capitalism as it is now practiced delivers the good life. Then there
are the political cadres within the Republican Party, who know how to combine patriotism, white resentment of people of color, and right-wing fundamentalist Christian fervor with long-standing antigovernment sentiments.
That mix creates a victorious voting coalition in enough rural districts and

southern and western states for Republicans to capture a majority of congressional seats and even the White House.

But pessimism is no more warranted than belief in inevitable victory. That's because no person or theory can predict the future. In 1988, just a few short years ago, no one would have believed that the Soviet Union, the second-most powerful country in the world, described as totalitarian and unchangeable by many scholars, would be transformed from inside with a minimum of bloodshed. Until that point, it was generally believed by those who study power that no ruling group would ever risk losing its power by trying large-scale changes, but that is exactly what Mikhail Gorbachev and his supporters did, even to the point of letting the East European satellite countries go their separate ways. Nor would it have been thought possible that the system of apartheid in South Africa could be dismantled without a murderous civil war, or that Nelson Mandela would be acknowledged as a great statesman and accepted by white South Africans in 1994 as their elected president.

Closer to home, no one would have imagined that a New Deal could emerge out of the Republican 1920s and the Great Depression, or that a moribund trade union movement could be revived at the same time through a combination of liberal legislation and courageous activism by rank-and-file leaders. Nor did anyone expect that a militant new civil rights movement would emerge from black churches and traditional black universities in the early 1960s, and only a few thought the movement could achieve its goals even after it had a full head of steam. This example is especially relevant because some of the leading liberals, moderates, and experts of the day opposed the sit-ins, freedom rides, and boycotts that sparked the necessary changes, or else cautioned the movement's leadership to proceed more slowly.

As these examples show, change can start tomorrow or fifty years from now. The challenge is to have the patience to stick with egalitarian values and be ready to act quickly if an unexpected opportunity arises. Egalitarians have always stood for trying to achieve what liberals timidly support, moderates fear is impossible, and elitists actively oppose. Thanks to their moral indignation and prodigious energy, they have been the catalysts for change even when the movements they supported eventually settled for far less than they thought desirable. This book suggests how today's egalitarians can continue this tradition of agitating for greater equality, fairness, and opportunity while preserving the personal, economic, and political rights won for all of us by their predecessors.

In effect, this book says that all the pieces are there for a strong egalitarian movement. But they have not been used effectively for two reasons. First, they have not been linked by an underlying rationale that shows activists how they all fit together. Second, they have been obscured and distorted by the inclusion of self-defeating methods that should not be part of the picture.

2

WHY EGALITARIANS SHOULD
TRANSFORM THE DEMOCRATIC PARTY

In the late nineteenth century, Belgium elected its parliament from geographical districts and had two stable political parties, with the Catholic Party usually defeating the Liberal Party. But in the 1890s a Socialist Party came on strong, and the Liberal Party was in danger of extinction. The Catholic Party quickly changed the electoral system because it did not want to end up in a one-on-one battle with the socialists. The system it chose, proportional representation, gave parties seats in the parliament roughly in proportion to their overall vote in the country as a whole. The Liberal Party was saved and Belgium operated with three political parties for many decades thereafter.

As this historical example suggests, electoral rules can play a big role in determining the number of parties. This possibility is confirmed by systematic studies comparing various kinds of electoral systems over the space of many decades. Electoral systems like the one Belgium used first, which are now designated by the overly long term mentioned in the previous chapter, single-member district plurality systems, almost always have just two parties. As also mentioned in chapter 1, the few third parties are usually regional or ethnic in nature. However, they are sometimes based on blue-collar workers and the few remaining radical small farmers.

In contrast to a system based on districts and pluralities, countries with systems of proportional representation usually have four or more parties, and would have even more if there weren't a minimum vote that had to be reached to receive any seats at all. Although the centrist parties soak up most of the votes, these countries are often governed by a coalition of two or more parties. Roughly speaking, there are left-of-center, center-left, center-right, and right-of-center coalitions. In this kind of system, everyone's vote counts, and voter turnout is therefore very high.

When it comes to electoral systems, the United States is the most extreme of the countries with a single-member district plurality system, meaning that its third parties have been very small and ephemeral. They rarely win more than 1 or 2 percent of the vote, and rarely last more than one or two elections when they do receive more than a few percent. This striking difference also is one key reason why so few socialists have been elected to Congress. In a study of the percentage of socialist or social democratic party members in national legislatures across the world, only South Africa had fewer—zero—than the two who made it to the U.S. House of Representatives a few times in the first quarter of the twentieth century. More leftists were elected to Congress in the 1930s and early 1940s as Democrats—from California, Washington, Montana, Minnesota, and New York—than were ever elected earlier as socialists. They weren't fully open about their socialism, or their sympathy for the Communist Party, but their views were well known to everyone involved in politics at the time.

The election of a president from the nation as a whole accounts for the even greater rigidity of the American two-party system. Control of the presidency, with its appointive and veto powers, and the expertise and budget powers at its command, is a huge prize that any political group with any pretensions of influence wants to win. Given the stakes involved, power brokers try to form preelection coalitions to see if they can reach a majority and ensure victory. In a parliamentary system with single-member districts, there is at least a little room for the creation of postelection coalitions between two parties, which is why new labor or socialist parties were able to grow quickly in England and northern Europe at the beginning of the last century.

At this point, the thought might occur that it would be possible to change the electoral system, as was done in Belgium and other countries due to the rise of labor and socialist parties. But the changes in Belgium and elsewhere were made by the dominant parties, not the insurgents, so such a change seems far less likely in the United States than making major alterations in the economic system. Even if the great majority of citizens wanted a system of proportional representation for the election of Congress as a whole, the Fifth Article of the Constitution says that "no State, without its consent, shall be deprived of its equal suffrage in the Senate," which means the small states could block any such change for the Senate. As far as the House, it is not going to happen there either because the citizens and politicians in the least populated states would lose a tremendous amount of political power. Even liberal Vermont, with a population of less than six hundred thousand, surely would line up with highly conservative states in the Great Plains because it would lose the only House seat it now has. Face it, the United States is tied to geographical units for choosing its Congress. That's because of the nature of the original colonization patterns, the Constitution, the expansion of the country westward, the huge geographical size of the country, historical sentiment, and on and on. Nor would it be possible to abolish the presidency and have a parliamentary system.

Now, it might be possible to convince the general public to go for a relatively simple change in the ballot that would allow for majority rule and more political parties. Under that plan, it would take a majority of the votes to win the office, and people would rank each candidate in order of preference. Then, if no candidate won a majority, the second choices of those who voted for the least successful candidate would be tallied, and so on until one candidate had a majority. It's called "instant runoff voting" and it is being tried, as you might guess, in San Francisco, thanks to a coalition including Common Cause, the National Organization for Women, the Sierra Club, the American Federation of Labor and Congress of Industrial Organizations, the Democratic Party, and the Green Party. With instant runoff voting, Ralph Nader supporters could have put Albert Gore Jr. second and Patrick Buchanan supporters could have put George W. Bush second, and Gore would have won by roughly 51 to 49 percent.

But right now it is Republicans and Democrats who control state legislatures and Congress, and it will be very difficult to convince them to risk their current power by adopting instant runoff voting for state and national elections. There's also the fact that people tend to treat the political system as far more sacred and unchangeable than the economic system. So if egalitarians are going to win any time soon, they are going to have to do so within the context of the current rules by taking over the Democratic Party and making changes in the economic system. They aren't the best rules for insurgents, but they are the hand that has been dealt. If activists can make progress with instant runoff voting, then more power to them, but it would take many years, and maybe decades, for them to get past the city, county, and state levels.

When some of the egalitarians of the past took a look at this frustrating situation, they decided the only way to alter it was to have a preliminary election for each party, which came to be called a primary. This system in effect allows leftists and liberals to duke it in out in one set of primaries, and moderate conservatives and ultraconservatives to go at it in the other set. Primaries were first instituted by reformers in Wisconsin in 1903 and then spread to the prairie states, where the northern European immigrants with socialist and radical farmer roots thought they were receiving a raw deal from corporations and big farmers. Primaries also came to be used in the South along about the same time by very different people for very different reasons—they were a way to exclude African Americans from power. These "white primaries," often operated under the fiction that they were merely a party function, were the final step in the disenfranchisement of African Americans in the late nineteenth century. They were not banned by the U.S. Supreme Court until 1944.

Either way, the primary system slowly spread and gained legitimacy, and by the 1970s it had almost completely replaced party conventions as a way of selecting delegates to the national conventions. Primaries were used as early as 1952 to challenge for the Democratic presidential nomination by Estes Kefauver, a maverick senator from Tennessee who opposed segregation in the South and the role of the Mafia in many Democratic machines in northern cities. He therefore was anathema to both groups, who backed Adlai Stevenson, an urbane corporate lawyer, in order to beat him at the party convention. Starting with the 1964 presidential candidacy of Senator Barry Goldwater of Arizona, right-wing Republicans began using primaries at all levels to increase their leverage within their party.

If cross-national comparisons and historical studies provide such a strong case against third parties, and if there are good structural reasons for making egalitarian challenges within the Democratic Party primaries, why is this approach so strongly, even vociferously, resisted by so many egalitarians, including the nation's most visible leftist scholars, many of whom enthusiastically endorsed Nader in 2000? Here my comments begin to take on a sharper edge.

Based on my reading and discussions with members of leftist third parties, I think there are several factors that explain the amazing persistence of a useless enterprise. The importance of each factor probably varies from person to person, but the net result is still the same, a small group of people who are determined that this time a leftist third party will work because they will do it right. At the most general level, this distaste for transforming the Democratic Party is a historical legacy of a time—pre-1970—when there were relatively few primaries and the party was controlled by northern urban bosses and racist southern white courthouse gangs. Except for liberal areas in a few northern states, there was no way egalitarians were going to go anywhere in the Democratic Party. The machine bosses in places like Chicago, Jersey City, and Kansas City probably would have had their Mafia friends rough up or run out of town any leftists foolhardy enough to challenge them. Entering southern white primaries in the face of the violence of the Jim Crow era was also out of the question.

Until as recently as the 1980s, then, the Democrats were first and foremost the party of the southern rich, who started it as a way to ensure that their plantation system and slavery would survive in the face of the growth of manufacturing in the North. At first, they found their allies among the landed rich of the rural North, such as on the vast estates of upstate New York, and later among the well-to-do Irish, Italian, and Jewish immigrants who made their money in real estate and related businesses in large northern cities. The northern rich, of course, had their own party, which was first the Federalists, then the Whigs, and then the Republicans since the 1850s.

Given the structural constraints on third parties, this arrangement meant there was no independent space for the northern-based liberal-labor coalition when it developed in the context of the New Deal. Despite its confinement within the Democratic Party, however, this coalition did manage to elect about one hundred Democrats to the House starting in the 1930s, where they joined with roughly one hundred southern Democrats and fifty machine Democrats to form a strong Democratic majority in all but a few sessions of Congress from 1934 to 1994. They were even able to pass some liberal spending legislation when they could convince the southern Democrats to join them.

But the picture was more negative when it came to issues concerning class interests. As early as 1938, the southern Democrats and northern Republicans formed a conservative voting bloc that stopped the liberal Democrats from passing legislation concerning union rights, civil rights, and the regulation of business, even when they could convince some machine Democrats to support them. These are precisely the issues that define class conflict in the United States. Civil rights fits that generalization because in the past such legislation really concerned keeping the African American workforce in the South from having any political power. The only way the liberal-labor coalition could pass measures like the National Labor Relations Act in 1935 was to give the southern Democrats what they wanted, namely, the exclusion of agricultural, seasonal, and domestic labor from its protections.

It might seem that the liberals would have found natural allies among the fifty machine Democrats from big urban areas like New York, Chicago, Boston, and Philadelphia, but more often than not they presented a liberal face to the public and then quietly sided with southern Democrats in private. They had impressive liberal voting records on legislation that made it to the floor, but they helped the southerners to gut such legislation behind the scenes and in committee. Most critically, the machine Democrats upheld the tradition of seniority and voted with the southerners in the party caucus, which meant that the southern Democrats controlled Congress thanks to the votes of fifty machine Democrats and the presence of the one hundred liberal Democrats who made the party a majority.

This remarkable bargain between the machines and the South at the expense of liberals and the urban working class was in part due to their similar backroom political styles, but they also shared a common interest in government spending to subsidize the enterprises of their backers. The basic deal was agricultural subsidies for southern plantation owners in exchange for housing and urban development subsidies in big cities. In addition, and this part of the bargain could not be spoken about publicly, they both shared an interest in keeping African Americans from voting. This desire to exclude blacks may sound surprising in the case of the machine politicians, but they actually feared that black voters would eventually replace them with black representatives, which turned out to be the case by the 1980s. Given this sordid pact at the heart of the Democratic Party, it is small wonder that older egalitarians with long memories have no hope of transforming the party and warn new egalitarians away from having anything to do with it.

Thus, the fact that Democrats dominated Congress between 1934 and 1994 was mostly irrelevant for those seeking egalitarian social change. Until the 1990s, the southerners could call the shots on class-oriented legislation through the conservative voting bloc with Republicans and control the Democratic Party through their alliance with the machine types. This is why it is a great mistake for liberal commentators and historians to talk about the "progressive" history of the party, meaning a few pieces of legislation in the mid-1930s and mid-1960s when egalitarian movements were generating serious social disruption.

But all this slowly began to change after 1965 thanks to the civil rights movement, a fact that is often overlooked by most of the egalitarians who continue to rail against the Democratic Party. It began to change because that movement not only brought rights and dignity to African Americans in the South, but it also undercut the disproportionate national power of the southern rich, which was based on dominating the Democratic Party by denying voting rights to African Americans as well as many low-income whites. Once African Americans won the right to vote in the South through the Voting Rights Act of 1965, they were able to help force out the worst racists by voting against them in Democratic Party primaries. At that point, the southern rich started to move over to the Republican Party, where they now felt more at home in any case due to the increasing industrialization of the South. Using appeals to racial resentment, religious fundamentalism, and social conservatism, they were able to take a majority of other whites along with them. Rich southern whites clearly knew how to construct and demonize an out-group in order to take the focus off class conflict.

However, this switch over was only gradual because the elected southern Democrats still had great power in Congress due to the seniority system for picking committee chairs. These "old bulls" hung on for as long as they could, only to be replaced by Republicans when they died or retired. At a certain point, though, when control of Congress seemed possible for the Republicans, some of these conservative Democrats suddenly switched parties while they were in office. The stage was thereby set for the Republican takeover in Congress in 1994.

The most immediate result of the Republicanization of the South was the breakup of the New Deal coalition at the presidential level, which relied on southern involvement far more than liberals like to remember. This breakup meant the election of Republican presidents from 1968 to 1976 and from 1980 to 1992. Even when the Democrats made their presidential comeback in 1992, it was through the efforts of a southern-based leadership group, the Democratic Leadership Council. In order to win, the rest of the Democrats accepted the council's two southern moderates, Bill Clinton and Gore, as their ticket because they knew they could not triumph without winning a few southern states. Clinton and Gore then hit all the right notes on religion, guns, and the death penalty to attract southern whites, and especially southern white males. They were better than Republicans on racial, feminist, and environmental issues, but not much else.

In the longer run, however, the civil rights movement had a much bigger impact on the structure of American politics. It freed the Democratic Party from inevitable control by conservatives. For the first time in American history, it became possible to create a nationwide egalitarian, liberal, labor,

African American, environmentalist, Hispanic, feminist, Asian American, and gay and lesbian coalition within the Democratic Party. Such a coalition has not been built for a number of reasons, including the fact that the most energetic egalitarians are not willing to join and the trade unionists are only recently becoming more hospitable to environmentalists, people of color, and feminists. But the potential is now there. Whether it ever will be used is another question.

For this left-of-center coalition to prevail, it has to win a majority in the House, sixty seats in the Senate (to cut off a filibuster), and place a moderate in the White House. This is a daunting challenge, of course. To succeed, it would have to do the difficult grassroots work of creating liberal black–white voting coalitions in the states of the Old South, which now have about 30 percent of congressional seats and 30 percent of the electoral votes. In other words, the same South that has always held the nation back due to its slave and Jim Crow past remains the biggest problem for egalitarians today. Think Newt Gingrich, Trent Lott, Tom DeLay, and George W. Bush, for example.

The transformation of the Democratic Party into an expression of a wide-ranging coalition pulled together by egalitarian activists could also decrease the importance of campaign finance in American politics. In the past, campaign donations have been critical to candidates in both primary and regular elections because of the need for name recognition and a unique image, thereby giving free-spending members of the capitalist class North and South a critical role in determining which candidates are likely to be successful. Money is not the only ingredient in a winning campaign, as the long list of well-financed losers demonstrates, but a certain large minimum usually is necessary to have much of a chance. This state of affairs has led many clean-money reformers to argue that limiting large donations is essential before liberal and left candidates can have a fair chance.

Short of a nationwide system of public financing for candidates, which seems highly unlikely in a Congress where Republicans from low-population states have a strong veto power in the Senate and great leverage in the House, it seems likely that wealthy "fat cats" will find one way or another to finance the candidates of their choice. Thus, the wiser course would be to concentrate on developing a strong and clear image for the Democratic Party so that it could rely on a core of loyalists who would vote for the party, not simply individual candidates. If the voters knew what the party consistently stood for, then the names, personalities, and images of individual candidates would be less important, and money would count for a whole lot less.

Since the Democratic Party has now shed its southern racist wing, and machine Democrats are mostly a thing of the past, it cannot be just historical memories that keep egalitarians from seeing the golden opportunity provided by party primaries. So something else must be going on as well. I think this something else is based in the strong moral sense that characterizes most egalitarian activists. Indeed, a moral outrage over the issues highlighted in egalitarian social movements is the most important thing they all share in common. It is an essential source of their energy and courage in facing great danger, but it can also be a hindrance because they cannot tolerate much compromise on the issues of concern to them, especially if they think people have failed to stand up for their beliefs. As speeches, articles, and letters to the editor by third-party advocates make abundantly clear, they see the Democrats as compromised, corrupt, and spineless. In this sense, egalitarians are "purists," and usually proud of it.

This moral zeal creates a strong inclination to separate from the everyday world and create an alternative set of standards and institutions. It generates a desire for a distinctive social identity and a space to call one's own, such as a third party. In addition, strong moral outrage creates a sense of immediacy that reinforces the preference for a third party as a way to express exasperation with compromise. As a result, egalitarians often become very annoyed with the liberal politicians who share most of their values and programs. As egalitarians say again and again, they want to be able to vote their "conscience," not the "lesser of two evils." The tensions that therefore arise between egalitarians and liberals within the electoral arena then become a hindrance to a general movement for egalitarian social change.

Moral indignation contributes to a preference for a third party in still another way. When changes do not come quickly, the activists' sense of frustration grows, especially when many of the people who are most exploited are slow to join the movement. The thought then arises that it takes strong medicine to "wake people up," to make them "realize" how badly they are being treated. What often follows is the conclusion that something drastic is necessary to shake people up, like a depression or a conservative Republican administration, so they can summon the energy to act in what egalitarians are sure are the best interests of the mistreated or downtrodden people they are trying to help. In short, they end up with a new theory: "The worse things are, the better the chances for egalitarian social change." Call it "the-worse-the-better theory."

The-worse-the-better theory combines with moral purism to create a preference for leftist third parties that supposedly will heighten the tensions by forcing people to face life under the harshest representatives of the capitalist class, the Republicans. In the context of a conflicted, cautious, and declining Democratic Party, it is thought that people will turn to the new third party as they grow weary of Republican rule. Contrary to this belief, egalitarians in the United States have done far better when moderates are in charge of the government because there is a greater possibility that social movements can have a positive effect on the political system. This is seen most dramatically during the New Deal, when union organizers were able to take advantage of mildly liberal labor legislation to create many new unions and pressure for the improved labor law that created the National Labor Relations Board in 1935. It is also shown by the fact that progressives did not prosper in the long winter of Reagan-Bush rule from 1981 to 1993.

The moral outrage that leads in the direction of third parties is understandable and admirable in the face of huge inequalities and unnecessary suffering, but there are better ways to express it and at the same time be more effective in the political arena. The first need is to make a distinction between activists and liberal politicians, and to see that they have different but complementary roles in bringing about egalitarian social change. Second, it is necessary to create a distinctive social identity and organizational space within the Democratic Party, not outside it.

Activists, to be effective, have to be uncompromising moralists who stand up for their principles. They are exemplars who break unjust laws when need be, and here of course the premier American examples are Martin Luther King Jr. and other leaders of the early civil rights movement. Although Nader does not break unjust laws and go to jail, saying he prefers "to be a plaintiff rather than a defendant," he is in fact a moral exemplar as well. He has sacrificed his everyday life to the civic causes he works on every hour of the day, using the money he makes from books and speeches to build new organizations that have had a measurable impact on the day-to-day lives of millions of Americans.

From their stance as movement activists, egalitarians constantly criticize mere "politicians." They lack courage and don't take enough principled stands. Activists therefore do not fully appreciate the role of elected officials as go-betweens, as tension reducers, as masters of timing and symbolism, and as people who want everyday life to go on once a particular election or argument has ended. Of course, they want to stay elected, and they deserve that bit of egoism, because they have gladly shaken the hands of thousands of people and listened to an earful to get where they are. Winning an elected office is not the kind of close-in emotional labor that very many people can tolerate unless they enjoy small talk, back patting, and endless arguments with people they hardly know or don't know at all.

Although most egalitarians think liberal politicians should just stand up for what they believe in and take the consequences, they are better thought of as the egalitarian activists' negotiators and diplomats within a democratic system. Yes, they should have strong liberal principles, but they also have to know when to do battle and when it is time to cut a deal. Their goal is to win the best they think possible for their side at any given moment and to be back for the next round. The crucial point for egalitarians is this: The liberals among politicians can only prosper when the egalitarian moral activists and their movements have made better deals possible, either by causing the election of more liberals or by forcing the moderates and conservatives to accept a deal they don't like in order to avoid losing the next election.

This interaction and mutual reinforcement between egalitarian activists and liberal politicians is the key to a new egalitarian movement. Progressive social change depends greatly on social movement organizations and strategic nonviolent actions outside the electoral area, but it requires an electoral dimension as well. Respecting the electoral dimension also requires that activists resist any temptation to take the hard-won democratic gains of the past for granted or even treat them with contempt. Egalitarians might like liberal politicians better if they thought of them as the defenders of the gains that have been made by egalitarians in the past. It was egalitarians in the nineteenth-century Populist Party, for example, who helped force the direct election of senators.

Perhaps needless to say, then, there are few moral activists who are also good politicians. The most striking exception is John Lewis, one of the truly great leaders of the early civil rights movement, who stood for principled nonviolence and therefore was ousted as the leader of the Student Nonviolent Coordinating Committee by Black Power advocates in 1965 when they ran out of patience with cautious white liberals and flawed trade unionists. Lewis recovered from that rejection and spent several years helping to register African American voters throughout the South. Then he won a seat on the Atlanta City Council in 1981 and an uphill battle for Congress in 1986.

Fortunately, there are a few people like Lewis who can bridge the gap between social movements and politics.

So what should egalitarian activists do in terms of future elections if and when the issues, circumstances, and candidates seem right? First, they should form egalitarian Democratic clubs (EDCs). This would give them an organizational base as well as a distinctive new social identity within the structural pathway to government that is labeled "the Democratic Party." Forming such clubs would make it possible for activists to maintain their sense of separatism and purity while at the same time allowing them to compete within the Democratic Party. There are numerous precedents for such clubs within the party, including liberal and reform clubs in the past, and the conservative Democratic Leadership Council at the present time.

This strategy of forging a separate social identity is also followed by members of the right wing within the Republican Party. By joining organizations like the Moral Majority and Christian Coalition, they can define themselves as Christians who have to work out of necessity within the debased confines of the Republican Party. That is, they think of themselves as Christians first and Republicans second, and that is what egalitarians should do, identify themselves primarily as egalitarians and only secondarily as Democrats.

After forming EDCs, egalitarian activists should find people to run in selected Democratic primaries from precinct to president. They should not simply support eager candidates who come to them with the hope of turning them into campaign workers. They have to create candidates of their own who already are committed to the egalitarian movement and to the programs that are suggested in the following chapters. The candidates have to be responsible to the clubs, or else the candidates naturally will look out for their own self-interest and careers. They have to focus on the planks in the platform and make no personal criticisms of their Democratic rivals. Personal attacks on mainstream politicians are a mistake, a self-made trap, for egalitarian insurgents.

In talking about the program, the candidates actually do much more than explain what egalitarians stand for. By discussing such issues as increasing inequality and the abandonment of fairness, and then placing the blame for these conditions on the corporate-conservative coalition and the Republican Party, they help to explain to fellow members of the movement who is "us" and who is "them." They help to create a sense of "we-ness," a new collective identity. As candidates who present a positive program and attack those who oppose it, they are serving as "entrepreneurs of identity," an important part of the job description for any spokesperson in a new social movement.

Since egalitarians are not likely to have the resources to run at all levels in all places, what are the best places to start when a good opportunity arises? One possibility is in Republican-dominated districts where it might be easy to take over moribund Democratic Party structures that do not try to put forward serious candidates. There are now many such House districts that might be ripe for the picking. Winning in Democratic primaries and then facing seemingly invincible Republican incumbents in the regular election may be more useful than it might seem at first glance. For example, when a progressive group in Michigan launched such a grassroots campaign in a Republican district in 1986, with the goal of sending the incumbent a message about his support for Reagan's militaristic foreign policy, their Democratic candidate received 41 percent of the vote, 10 percent higher than the previous Democratic challenger. Such a large vote on the first try would be a wonderful starting point if it could be achieved in the same election year in a number of districts and states where the regular Democrats already had conceded the election to the Republicans.

It also makes sense to run candidates at the congressional level in a few highly Democratic districts, where an egalitarian might have a real chance of winning the regular election if he or she could win the primary. These opportunities might arise when incumbent Democrats vacate their seats in districts where grassroots activists have established a strong record through their nonelectoral efforts. They would be entering primaries in which there would likely be several candidates splitting the moderate vote. Since the turnout is often low in primaries, a highly organized egalitarian campaign that fully mobilized all of its potential supporters would have some solid possibilities.

As for the presidential level, a focus on one well-known activist with good egalitarian credentials might be worthwhile if the campaign was used to develop EDCs and other party-transforming activities. Absent such a person, different candidates could be fielded on the same platform in different regions of the country or in selected states such as New York, Massachusetts, Oregon, and California. That way, the effort could be made without having to raise huge amounts of money.

For example, a John Lewis or some other prominent liberal African American leader with political experience as an elected official might be able to win the Super Tuesday primaries across the southern states, thereby heightening the visibility and strengthening the role of African Americans in the egalitarian wing of the party. It is often overlooked that Jesse Jackson won the most votes overall in this string of same-day primaries when they were first held in 1988, thanks for the most part to the African American vote. And if enough different presidential candidates were able to win delegates in a range of states, then it might be possible for egalitarian Democrats to have a role in the Democratic National Convention, which has been reduced in recent decades to a ceremonial occasion and media extravaganza. Perhaps the delegates could even play a part in choosing the vice presidential candidate.

Egalitarian candidates invariably will be asked if they are out to win or expect to win, and the answer should be "yes, but only on our own terms," which means that winning is only worthwhile if voters are endorsing the egalitarian platform and expressing a sense of identification with the egalitarian movement. Thus, there can be no thought of trimming on one or another part of the agreed-on platform with the hope of squeaking by. Otherwise, the whole political effort loses it sense of collectivity and turns back into an individualistic contest based on name recognition and personality.

However, once a highly principled campaign has been waged and the egalitarian challengers lose, as most of them surely would the first few times out, then they should congratulate the winners and announce their support for them in the regular election. Then they should return to work in the social movement of their choice. How they vote in the privacy of the polling booth is their own business, of course, but their public stance should be resolutely pro-Democrat.

If the insurgents are likely to lose, what is the purpose of the exercise? I am sure you know the answers to that question by now, so I only need to list them fairly quickly:

- Insurgent campaigns in Democratic primaries provide an opportunity to introduce new ideas and programs into the political arena at a time and place when the most politically active citizens are paying at least a little bit of attention.
- By defining the group in terms of its opposition to the corporate-conservative coalition, insurgent campaigns help to forge a sense of collective identity, a sense of "we-ness." As I will explain more fully in chapter 5, an egalitarian Democrat identity is needed as an addition to, not a replacement for, the strong social identities that are already held by the various groups in the coalition.
- The reactions of voters to these new policy proposals provide an

opportunity to hone and refine them so they better suit the needs of those they are designed to serve.

- Insurgent campaigns provide an opportunity to recruit new activists who are attracted by the new programs.
- Such campaigns provide egalitarian candidates with much-needed experience in the political arena that could come in very handy at a later date, when there is greater sympathy for an egalitarian program. This experience also keeps candidates and their activist supporters from separating themselves and from disparaging the overwhelming number of people who are nonactivists.
- Insurgent campaigns are a chance to gauge the degree of support for egalitarian programs. Anything higher than the few tenths of a percent won by left-wing third parties in regular elections in recent decades would be a big moral victory.
- If the vote total is high enough, it gives egalitarians leverage with elected Democrats. It should not be forgotten that it was Jesse Jackson's impressive vote totals in Democratic primaries in 1984 and 1988 that earned him access to the White House in the 1990s. Jackson's campaigns were a disappointment and failure in that he was not really interested in building an organization that was independent of his own career. But that doesn't negate the fact that he won more votes in the primaries in 1988 than Gore, which is a big reason why Clinton and Gore were careful to consult with him throughout their years in office. They didn't want him out there running against them.

NADER EXPLAINS THE NADER CAMPAIGN

Thanks to a highly detailed postelection book that Nader wrote to chronicle and justify his 2000 presidential campaign as a candidate of the Green Party, it is possible to see how well the critique in this chapter applies to this most recent incarnation of the egalitarians' quest for their own third party.

Nader's main claim is that the two parties are increasingly the same, and thus there is a need for a new third party that offers voters a real choice. This claim has two dimensions to it. First, the Democrats are far worse than their liberal supporters imagine. They have been collapsing on major issues since the 1970s, forsaking their "progressive" past, and matters only got worse in the Clinton-Gore years. Nader delivers a detailed indictment of these Democratic failures, including all the rejections of his own efforts by Gore and even the Progressive Caucus in the House.

Second, and even more important in terms of justifying a third party, Nader argues that the Republicans are not as dangerous as the liberal Democrats claim. George W. Bush is not exactly "Genghis Khan," as he notes at one point and then lists the various ways Bush moved to the center in his first year in office. Nader also reminds critics that "the liberals' arch-reactionary," Richard M. Nixon, signed the laws creating the Environmental Protection Agency and the Occupational Safe and Health Administration in 1970, and used "glowing words" in doing so, thanks to the pressure from the strong social movements of the 1960s that still existed when Nixon was in his first term. He counters the liberal fear of Republican appointments to the Supreme Court by doubting that any court would risk overturning *Roe v. Wade,* and by naming several Republican judicial appointees of the past thirty-two years who have turned out to be fair-minded on the right to choose issue.

Nader's lack of deep concern when contemplating a Republican presidency is very different from the usual egalitarian view of Republicans as their main opponents. It can be appreciated more fully when it is contrasted with right-wing views of the Democrats. Due to their abhorrence of "big government," labor unions, and/or liberal social values, right wingers generally avoid third parties at all costs because they genuinely fear the Democrats as the worst of all out-groups. A Clinton or a Gore looks tame to left-wing third-party advocates, but not to right wingers, who believe that the Democratic coalition, with Clinton and Gore representing its moderate wing, spells trouble for their worldview. Gore is Genghis Khan to conservatives, but Bush is not Genghis Khan to most left activists, including Nader, and therein lies an important part of the political equation in America. The energy of zealous right-wing activists is used on behalf of the Republicans, thereby uniting all those who are right of center when they step into the political arena, but the great energies and moral fervor of the egalitarians are often used in attacking Democrats as sell-outs, leaving those who are left of center divided among themselves and often demoralized.

But it is not only that the two parties are about the same according to Nader. He also makes a case that it is useful for the Democrats to lose if activist groups are to be energized enough to realize their goals through nonviolent direct action and lobbying pressure. Democrats take activist groups for granted once the activists endorse them, and the activists tend to sit back when Democrats are in office. The result, says Nader, is disastrous. The Democrats put activists to sleep; they "anesthetize" activists. Thus, he argues that activist groups often do better when the Democrats are not in power.

Furthermore, he continues, it may be good for the Democrats to lose once in a while so that they don't take the citizen groups and social movements for granted. This is necessary because "[t]he only message politicians understand is losing an election." This comes fairly close to saying that it was time to sink Gore, especially when read in the context of the many extremely negative things he has to say about Gore on a wide variety of issues, and most pointedly environmental issues. Here, Nader's reasoning seems to be a mild version of the-worse-the-better theory.

The likelihood that Nader wanted to cost Gore the election also can be seen in the fact that he chose to go to Miami to campaign the Saturday before the election. He says that's because he hadn't spent much time in Florida, but he did so knowing the race was very close there, and despite the fact that some of his political scientist and sociologist supporters wanted him to draw back in Oregon, Wisconsin, and Florida to ensure a Gore victory in those crucial states. I take up the dark possibility that Nader was out to destroy Gore, not build a third party, when I discuss the issue of domination by strong leaders in chapter 6.

Nader also claims there are virtues to third parties. They introduce new issues and bring out new voters, some of whom vote for Democrats in races where the third party does not have candidates. He claims there were a million new voters in 2000 thanks to his campaign, and takes credit for the victory of Democratic senatorial candidate Maria Cantwell in the state of Washington, where she won by twenty-three hundred votes over the incumbent Republican. He also draws on the relative successes of the third-party presidential campaigns by John Anderson in 1980 and H. Ross Perot in 1992 and 1996 to support his brief for third parties.

Although Nader's specific arguments about the Democrats and Republicans have their merits, they do not address the structural problem that he understands; instead, he discusses them as a mere "obstacle" to be overcome in the slow process of building a movement and a third party. He does not admit that the everyday, short-run interests of the supporters of the Democratic Party, such as low-income workers, women who work outside the home, disadvantaged people of color, and religious liberals, are likely to be ignored as more and more Republicans assume office while the third party is being built. Nader reduces the argument over third parties to questions about being a "spoiler" in relation to the Democratic *candidate,* when the real issue is that there is no way to build a third party without damaging the interests of the *everyday people* who vote for the Democratic Party as a way of trying to make small gains or just stay even while living their normal lives. Nader earned his deserved reputation fighting for small victories that make people's lives better, but he opts for sacrificing their everyday interests when he turns to the electoral arena.

Bush may not be Genghis Khan, but he and his fellow Republicans will resist matters like union rights, abortion rights, clean energy, affirmative action, global warming, workplace safety and health, protections for gays and lesbians, habitat preservation, and increases in the minimum wage far more vigorously than Democrats would during the many years it would take, by Nader's own account, to build this new third party. They therefore deserve to be taken far more seriously as the main political arm of the corporate-conservative coalition that opposes an egalitarian movement. Perhaps the Republicans would soon overreach in their reactionary efforts on taxes, social security, and the environment, leading to the citizen outcry that Nader believes will restrain them. But it is unlikely that any Republican-induced economic downturns or scandals would lead to anything useful because there would not be enough moderates and liberals in Congress to accomplish significant reforms. Even when economic downturns and corporate scandals provide opportunities for liberals and moderates to act, they may not be able to muster the energy to try for reforms because Bush is sitting there with a veto and with the ability to appeal to patriotism and white pride if he feels threatened in 2004. The progressive "backlash" that Nader hopes for won't happen without more liberal and moderate Democrats in office, but his third-party strategy works against Democrats winning elections.

In addition, as explained earlier in the chapter, it is not accurate to assert that the two parties are becoming more and more similar. They actually have become increasingly different over the past thirty-five years. Nader romanticizes the "progressive" past of the Democrats by ignoring something he well knows from his own uphill battles in Washington, that the party was controlled until the 1970s by white southern conservatives and their friends in many large northern cities. It was not the party of liberals and labor, who had to take a back seat except when the union movement of the 1930s and the civil rights movement of the 1960s gave them some temporary leverage. Nor does he emphasize that the civil rights movement and the Voting Rights Act of 1965 actually changed the two-party system dramatically by making it possible for southern black voters to push southern white conservatives into the Republican Party. There are now very few Democrats who are as conservative as the most "liberal" of Republicans, unlike the situation as late as the 1980s. True, the political spectrum has moved to the right on many economic issues, but the parties themselves never have been more different. At the voter and congressional levels, the Democrats are now the party of those who believe in fairness and equality whatever their own social backgrounds, or who have been marginalized or treated badly in some way.

Nader refers to the support received by Anderson in 1980 and Perot in 1992 and 1996 as evidence for the possibilities of third parties, but their candidacies are irrelevant from an egalitarian point of view because they came from the center, not the left or right, and therefore were not greeted by Democrats and Republicans with the same anxiety and anger as a party like Nader's. Nader tries to counter this kind of argument by saying that he also drew votes from centrists and Republicans, but that argument is not at all convincing or reassuring to the Democrats when they look at the politics of the activists, academics, and celebrities who supported Nader. It is as certain as such things can be that a left third party takes more votes from Democrats than Republicans, and therefore helps Republicans.

Nader claims third parties are the way new ideas come into the political arena, but most of his examples are from the nineteenth century, before reformers gradually created primaries, which in fact have been the main source of new programs since World War I. His main twentieth-century example is the claim by Ted Koppel on *Nightline* that Socialist Party presidential candidate Norman Thomas introduced the idea of Social Security during the 1928 campaign. That inaccurate claim only shows that Koppel knows nothing about the origins of the Social Security Act, which was fashioned in the early 1930s by moderate conservatives from companies like Standard Oil of New Jersey, General Electric, and Eastman Kodak, with the help of hired experts paid by John D. Rockefeller Jr. and his foundations, and then promoted by centrists and liberals in the Democratic Party.

Nader sees nonvoters as a prime target for a new third party, but solid studies of nonvoters suggest that they are not much different in their views from voters, even though they tend to have somewhat lower incomes or less education. They are not any sort of natural leftists or progressives due to their social standing, and are probably as likely to vote their skin color, their religion, or their ethnicity as any other voter. Contrary to Nader, the trick is to start with the most involved egalitarians, the left activists and liberal Democrats, and then reach out to moderates and nonvoters, but that cannot be done through a third party because it immediately divides the leftists and the liberals against each other.

Like other egalitarians, Nader constantly denigrates politicians in very strong moral terms, reserving special venom for the liberals and moderates. By showing little respect for the politician's craft, and thereby ignoring the need for both activists and politicians, Nader inadvertently strays from his democratic starting point and ends up with an elitist electoral stance contrary to his values. In a word, he thinks he knows better than the great mass of people who voted their short-run interests through the politicians of the Democratic Party. This is somewhat ironic, of course, because his most notable successes as an activist involved small gains that benefited a great many people.

In fact, in reaction to the many egalitarian critics of his campaign, he boasts about most of these small victories at one point or another, using them as evidence that the feminists, civil rights leaders, environmentalists, and labor leaders who vehemently attacked him should have supported him because he has a better record on their issues than Gore. When it comes to elections, though, most people do not believe they should sacrifice their everyday lives for a cause that they don't think has a chance in the world to succeed. Most Americans intuitively understand the structural argument against third parties of the left or right, and that is why they won't have anything to do with them, even though most of these people respect and appreciate what Nader has done as an activist over the years.

Contrary to the highly positive assessment Nader makes of his 2000 campaign, it is more likely that it will go down in history as the biggest electoral setback for leftists, radicals, socialists, progressives, environmentalists, and other egalitarian insurgents since the Henry Wallace defeat of 1948. It expended an enormous amount of activist time and energy to put Nader on the ballot in forty-three states, only to end up with 2.7 percent of the vote, less than half of the 6 to 7 percent he anticipated. It also created a legacy of bitter liberal elected officials who will do everything they can to isolate him and the Green Party even further. He also has alienated many liberal environmentalists, feminists, and civil rights leaders. Whether he likes it or not, his effort will be remembered as the first leftist campaign that ever affected the outcome of a presidential election.

If Nader and his energetic forces had been Green or egalitarian Democrats in 2000, running openly on their "ten key values," which include a commitment to strategic nonviolence, they would have gained some of the legitimacy needed to take advantage of the economic disasters visited on millions of people by the collapse of the dot-com bubble, the terrorist attacks on September 11, 2001, and the Enron scandal. Instead, Nader and his supporters ignored the structural realities of the electoral system and opted for a strategy that was bound to hurt and anger liberal Democrats, taking the chance that such a strategy might reenergize grassroots groups and force Democratic candidates to take egalitarian issues more seriously.

It is not easy to have all the pieces in place for a chance at establishing an egalitarian toehold in the electoral system. There has to be the right combination of issues, momentum, and candidates. The Nader campaign inspired hope among many activists precisely because of his strong egalitarian credentials and high visibility, and he had a number of good issues due to growing corporate domination, the increasing concentration of the wealth and income distributions, and the poor record of mainstream politicians on the environment. That is why the failed campaign was such a waste. It squandered political and moral capital that is very hard for egalitarians to accumulate. His refusal to take the results of social science and historical studies seriously destroyed his credibility as a thoughtful person. He left many of his followers confused or disillusioned, while at the same time hardening the moralistic sense of superiority of the handful who remain loyal to his causes.

So to avoid all these problems, and contrary to conventional egalitarian thinking, this chapter has presented a new strategy that should be followed within the political process. But what are the underlying principles of a program that could be presented by egalitarian Democrats in party primaries? What is the message beyond criticizing corporations and exposing the weaknesses of the policy proposals put forth by mainstream Democrats and the Republicans?

3

MORE EQUALITY THROUGH
THE MARKET SYSTEM

We don't need blueprints," a leading activist-scholar told a left-friendly audience in the early months of 2001. Like so many, she thinks it is best to simply jam, hassle, and disrupt in order to force the authorities to respond. "There are no solutions, just reforms." She thinks of herself as a "movement person."

Well, I think she is mostly wrong. I say "mostly" instead of "totally" because you cannot develop a complete blueprint; any thought of creating a detailed utopian vision can only fail, as many historical attempts decisively show. However, it is possible to establish the key principles on which the economic system should operate, and then develop and fight for the programs that implement those principles in specific areas, like on health care, working conditions, and unemployment insurance, to take three areas where major improvements would make a great deal of difference in millions of people's lives. But it is precisely on the issue of a plausible vision for a better economic future that egalitarians have been totally lacking since the collapse of socialism as a believable alternative. Although they have set forth many specific policy proposals, they have not been able to project a new set of principles to inspire and guide positive changes in the economic system. This is a defect that few activists have been willing to face. It is right up there with third parties as a reason for ongoing egalitarian failure.

Whether it is realized or not, Marxian theory has had a big impact on this debate about the need for "blueprints" because it is very negative toward them. This skepticism goes back to the days in the 1840s when Karl Marx and Friedrich Engels scorched the mere "utopian socialists" as advocates of political wishful thinking with their demonstration communities, model factories, and appeals to reason. Societies don't change just because a few people have shown there may be a better way to do things, they argued. Societies are power structures constituted by rival social classes and their political and cultural allies, so the leaders of the working class have to have a program that is consistent with the unfolding logic of capital. For example, working-class advocates of "small is beautiful" would not get very far because the competitive logic of capitalism leads inevitably to fewer and fewer increasingly large concentrations of capital that are now called multinational corporations.

Since the contradictory inner workings of capitalism make socialism inevitable, capitalism is doomed, and its exploited workers are the ones who are going to transform it. It's a complicated story, and today's Marxists disagree among themselves concerning some of the details about how capitalism will fail. But this eventual collapse means there is no need to present a full-scale alternative economic program. It is enough to explain that socialism consists of public or government ownership of large income-producing enterprises, perhaps supplemented by consumer and worker cooperatives. These socialized enterprises would be operated for the benefit of everyone through a system of central planning responsible to democratically elected officials.

However, a vague outline of a social system called socialism is not the only blueprint on which the Marxists actually built. They also benefited from the reservoir of hope for socialism created by the utopian experiments and utopian socialist authors they criticized. Moreover, they had an even more powerful blueprint, a blueprint for the logic of history itself. The idea that socialism is inevitable is in itself a powerful alternative blueprint, a vision of inevitable improvement. Since the workers of the world would eventually unite and overthrow capitalism out of necessity, Marxists were only organizing to speed things along. History was on their side.

Due to the influence of this theory, some activists still maintain that there is no need for blueprints. They therefore feel confident in saying that it is only necessary to stir people into action around some issue, such as the need for unions, and then they will come to see the necessity for socialism as they realize that capitalism is completely opposed to their values and goals. This tendency to downplay the need for an alternative vision for the future was reinforced by the economic and political failures of the Soviet

Union and China, which made any discussion of socialism even more unattractive to average Americans. Although Marxists blamed these difficulties on the previous lack of economic development in those countries, combined with the hostile actions toward them by capitalist countries, they still couldn't use such backward and undemocratic countries as shining examples of the socialist future when trying to win the allegiance of Americans. Moreover, by the 1980s it became clear that a centrally planned economy wouldn't work very well even after considerable industrial development and decades of experience with planning. This failure cannot be attributed to a lack of democracy, as some theorists now argue. The problems are economic and sociological, not political. The general failure of a centrally planned economy is a major turning point in the egalitarian project because it calls socialism into question as the way to realize egalitarian values.

Why is it so hard for many activists to let go of the unworkable idea of central planning as the key to a more egalitarian social system? It is because of the extremely negative view of the market in Marxist theory. The market is first of all seen as too impersonal and too conducive of competitiveness. It reduces all human relationships to an individualistic "cash nexus," which is nearly the opposite of the collective human values implied by "from each according to their abilities, to each according to their needs." Then, too, the impersonal market is a snare and a delusion because it is the most pernicious method ever devised to legitimate the exploitation of labor. The wage relationship in a market system conceals the extent to which people are working for nothing a good part of the day. Workers are led to believe that they are receiving a fair day's wage for a fair day of work, but in fact they are being screwed due to the fact that their lack of capital forces them into the labor market and puts them at the mercy of what a capitalist is willing to pay. The capitalist then takes the surplus value created by the worker—the value over and beyond what it takes to feed workers and their families—and "realizes" it as a profit. The capitalist then uses this profit to live the good life and invest in order to make more profit. This central theoretical point is summarized by the following phrase: The "exploitation" of workers is disguised as "commodity exchange."

Thus, there is a need for a centrally planned economy because working for a wage to produce a product for sale on the market is inherently alienating and exploitative. "Market socialism," in which markets are used in conjunction with some degree of central planning and public ownership of productive enterprises, is not acceptable either because it still leaves workers at the mercy of economic laws. The creative and productive energies that uniquely characterize human beings are crushed and crippled by any wage system whatever the form of ownership. "Capitalism," says the current editor of the *Socialist Register,* "is unjust and undemocratic not just because of this or that imperfection in relation to equality or freedom, but because at its core it involves the control by some of the use and development of the potential of others and because the competition it fosters frustrates humanity's capacity for liberation through the social." The few theorists who argue for a market socialism are therefore seen by most Marxists as abandoning the very heart of the Marxian analysis and vision.

But central planning does not work economically and has strong authoritarian tendencies built into it that do not promote freedom. It first of all fails economically because no one has been able to design methods to analyze the tremendous amount of information necessary to manage a large-scale centrally planned economy that goes beyond a few core industries. It also fails economically and politically because the large bureaucratic system created to try to obtain and utilize this information becomes completely inefficient and corrupt in the way many such large organizations often do. The leaders use their positions to feather their own nests. They get into power struggles with each other that make the system even more unwieldy. They look out for their friends and relatives, which lowers the competence levels. Managers have to buy on the black market, cut corners, and cheat in order to meet their production quotas, which increases corruption, destroys morale, and dampens any desire to work better and harder for the sake of the collective good. Managers also adulterate goods and ignore the effects of their production processes on the environment, leading to greater pollution than in market systems. The more complex the economy becomes, the worse the planning problems become. Inefficiency, waste, corruption, lack of innovation, and environmental degradation were the hallmarks of the Soviet Union and other efforts at central planning.

Thus, as harsh and undemocratic as communist regimes are, they do not fail for political or military reasons. In both the Soviet Union and China, for example, political and military control was intact when they embarked on changes in their economies in an attempt to overcome the difficulties inherent in central planning. They failed because their economies were faltering, which in turn caused a very large morale problem by forcing the realization that central planning is not a sound basis for building a more productive and egalitarian society. In other words, and this assertion is crucial, the Soviet Union would have failed as a socialist society even if it had been democratic because central planning would have undermined the economy. This is the lesson of recent historical experience that has been the hardest for many egalitarians to face. Indeed, the lesson is so severe that it is doubtful that even a hybrid like market socialism could prosper because it too relies on a considerable degree of central planning. In addition, it puts too much power in government agencies by giving them ownership of large-scale enterprises, which creates an imbalance opposite to the one that now exists in the United States.

If central planning is a disaster and markets are primarily instruments for exploitation, then it is no wonder that egalitarian activists have not been able to project the necessary vision of a better future that would provide renewed energy for their work. It is understandable that they would simply say that the current system is not good enough, but not offer any alternatives. However, there is actually more hope than most egalitarians realize. While many leftists have been busy criticizing modern-day economics as an exercise in producing irrelevant mathematical formulas, a new generation of economists has shown that the idolization of the market as a perfect, impersonal, and self-regulating mechanism that always leads to the best possible outcomes is as far from reality as the hopes of socialist central planners. The claims by free market ideologues that any laws regulating the market hinder productivity, or that greater economic equality inevitably limits freedom, are without significant empirical support. Research shows that markets need guidance from government to operate well, and that there is no inevitable trade-off between equality and efficiency, or between equality and freedom, within a market system. More equality might even mean more efficiency, not less, and it can certainly mean more freedom for more people.

Most importantly for our purposes, markets can be reconstructed to make it possible to plan for a more egalitarian economic future. It turns out it is possible for strong governments to use the market system for planning. Once it is realized that markets can be viewed from a governmental point of view as administrative instruments for planning, it can be seen that with a little reconfiguring they can serve collective purposes as well as the individual consumer preferences trumpeted by conservative free market economists. In this form of planning, the information is supplied by the price system that is so central to the considerable, but far from perfect, efficiency brought about by markets.

There is thus no need for one big planning apparatus. Instead, the planning tools within a reconstructed market system are simply taxes, subsidies, government purchases, and regulation. This point may seem very mundane, but these well-known government powers can be potent when applied to markets. They make it possible to speak in terms of restructuring the market system. They make it possible for different agencies of the state to tinker with different parts of the economic system and to change course quickly if the economy does not respond as projected. In the past, egalitarians could not think of these interventions as planning tools for two reasons. First, they are currently used by the corporations that dominate the government for their own short-run interests. Second, most egalitarians couldn't see the possibilities for any kind of decentralized market planning because they thought of planning as central planning.

The annual battle over energy policy in Congress can be seen in this light as an exercise in planning through the market, and as a prototype for the kind of policy struggles that could be waged on other issues. The environmentalists call for higher taxes on fossil fuels, subsidies for renewable energy sources, and regulations that force automobile manufactures and utilities to burn fuels more efficiently and cleanly. They ask the government to purchase heating and cooling systems that use renewable energy for its buildings and to use vehicles that meet the highest standards of fuel efficiency. On the other hand, the oil, coal, automobile, and utility companies demand low taxes on fossil fuels, subsidies for fossil fuels, and minimal or no regulations relating to efficiency or pollution, which in effect is a very different plan. If the environmentalists' plan were to prevail, the United States could gradually wean itself from foreign oil and clean up the air and water at the same time.

Planning through the market is, in effect, the general strategy adopted by the environmental movement, and it has paid good dividends. Although most environmental programs actually increase the number of jobs, not decrease them, the plans developed by environmentalists can call for the government to subsidize any job losses or sudden dislocations through "just transition" programs. For example, in a 2002 plan developed for a green-blue alliance, which would reduce carbon emissions by half in 2020, the authors include a proposal for two years of income and up to four years of education for those who lose their jobs, along with $10,000 in community funds for each job lost. At the same time, they note that their plan to tax carbon and increase the use of renewable energy sources would increase the overall number of jobs. "Just transitions" would be financed by everyone through their taxes, which is a collective solution to a collective problem.

According to this new way of thinking about planning, then, the big issue is winning political power from the corporate-conservative coalition, which is another reason why challenges in the electoral arena are such an important dimension of a full-scale egalitarian movement within a democratic society. That is, taxes, subsidies, government purchases, and regulations could be used by egalitarians to do planning through the market if they had enough power in the government. The economic issues are not all that arcane. The solutions are there. But the political power has been sorely lacking.

Nor is it necessary that corporations have all the rights of real persons they now enjoy under American law thanks to the governmental power their owners have exercised. They need not be able to enter into the political arena as if they were actual people. Their charters could be limited to the legal rights that are needed for them to buy, sell, and manage a workforce.

Once markets are accepted as a necessity for the production and distribution of most products and services, it is possible to really hammer home on the areas where they don't work the way politically conservative free market economists say they do. Here, there is much support from moderate and liberal economists. Even the most extreme of free marketers, the libertarians, admit that there are "market failures." For example, some of them will grant that there are four instances where nonmarket solutions have what they call a higher level of payoff than private spending. They're talking about education, public sanitation, mass transit, and highways, which together cover plenty of territory and provide a good starting point.

There is of course much more than those four areas that are not well served by the market, such as the justice system, parks, and support for the disabled and elderly, which are already under the domain of government. None of these past gains would be lost. However, by realizing that the market is the starting point for the production of most goods and services, and then talking in terms of "planning through the market," "market failures," and "reconstructing the market," egalitarians gain an enormous ideological advantage. They make it possible to think more expansively and creatively about what government agencies can do within the economy instead of worrying about the possibility that government bureaucracies may become too big and oppressive. They also disarm the conservatives at the theoretical level. They force them to talk about specific cases—all crucial to social well-being—where even the conservatives' own economists have conceded that the market is less than perfect. In fact, the free marketers' admission about a "higher level of payoff" from nonmarket solutions in some cases can be used as a mantra to move on to other market failures. Important issues in social life where the market cannot get values right can also be used as a battering ram against the antigovernment ideology of low taxes that is employed by the corporate-conservative coalition to stifle government spending for the social services everyone needs and wants.

For example, the whole area of health care is another instance of "market failure" for a variety of reasons. People don't have the time or expertise to shop around when they are sick, so it is difficult to have much "consumer choice." No one could possibly save enough to pay for the care needed during a catastrophic illness. Not just anyone can deliver health care, so there are "barriers to entry." Most of all, of course, health care providers cannot make a profit if they have to treat people who cannot pay, which means they would have to let such people sicken or die instead of helping them. The result in the United States is an inefficient private insurance system with a bigger bureaucracy than the government would have if all the bills were paid by Medicare. There are other areas of life where traditional ideas about markets don't make much sense either, but it is not my purpose to suggest a detailed set of programs. My focus here, as elsewhere in the book, is on basic principles and processes. The important point for now is that a critique of the weaknesses in the market system has more credibility if it is within the context of understanding that centralized planning is hopeless.

By drawing on the experience of other democratic capitalist countries, it is also possible to show convincingly that a reconstructed market system could be much more open and flexible than the one that currently exists in the United States. For example, it is possible to have many different types of enterprises compete in the market, not just privately owned corporations. It is possible to conceive of a fully functioning market system based on consumer-owned cooperatives, or of state-owned firms, or a combination of cooperative, state-owned, and private companies. At the least, agencies of the government can own companies that could enter into highly concentrated markets and provide competition for the oligopolists. This is in essence what the New Deal did when it created the Tennessee Valley Authority to produce electricity and fertilizer for the underdeveloped areas along the Tennessee River. The price-gouging utilities controlled by holding companies in New York protested mightily, but the southern Democrats saw them as Yankee exploiters, and that was the end of it.

Needless to say, a reconstructed market would not put an end to the wage system, so it would not satisfy those influenced by classical Marxist theory. It would not deal with the desire to abolish competition and concentrate on creating more opportunities for self-development within the context of greater nonmarket social cooperation. But planning through the market could be used to decrease the degree of exploitation that currently exists by making wages higher, the work process more humane, and employment in some form or another a political right. Better unemployment benefits and guaranteed health insurance in one form or another would also reduce exploitation through the wage system.

Within this context, it might be possible for those who decry the alleged alienation created by markets to think about the fact that a majority of Americans express satisfaction with their jobs even under present conditions, suggesting that they would find them even more positive in a reconstructed market system with genuine protections for working people. It might also be possible to consider the most general theoretical point that can be made about a market system: It is first and foremost a general social system that makes it possible to have coordination through mutual adjustments. It is a form of cooperation in which people do not have to attend a series of meetings beforehand, or enter into lengthy discussions, or even like each other. There are elements of coercion, in the sense that people have to work at a job for a wage, but they would have to do that in a centrally planned economy, too, for many, many decades.

There are also interesting ways to level up incomes through the market because capitalists are more willing to accept support programs for low-income people that do not interfere with markets for low-wage labor. This means, for example, that they do not object as strenuously to year-end government supplements to the wages of those who have worked a prescribed number of hours at a low-wage job. This supplement is now known by the euphemism "earned income tax credit" (EITC), but it also has been called a "negative income tax." From the point of view of workers, it is a year-end bonus from the government. From the point of view of capitalists, it is a government subsidy. From the point of view of egalitarians and government, it is a way to create greater income equality in exchange for accepting the discipline of the market.

The EITC has been endorsed by both free market and left-liberal economists, and it was not stopped by the conservative voting bloc in Congress. It has helped significant numbers of low-wage workers, some of whom receive advance payments. The program is currently restricted to single workers who make less than $11,000 a year working a specified number of hours, and to married workers with two or more children who make less than roughly $32,000 a year. However, now that the principle behind the program is accepted, pressure could be mounted to improve the program so that everyone over the age of eighteen who works the minimum number of hours would be boosted to a living wage. All of this could be paid for through a more progressive income tax, which would signify a collective commitment to greater income equality.

The heresy of this chapter for egalitarians is to admit that markets can have the virtue of being a decentralized form of coordination and control that does expand opportunity for most people. Yes, they can also make it possible for the owners of income-producing private property to gain the power to dominate government, as is currently the case in the United States. But by their very nature they leave open the possibility that government can limit the power and rewards of ownership through taxes, subsidies, government purchases, and regulation. Government can also create competitive public enterprises to compete with privately owned companies and tax incomes and wealth far more than it is doing now without disturbing the functioning of the market.

On balance, then, markets are more useful than not and can provide a starting point for developing new egalitarian policies and programs that have only been touched on briefly in this chapter. It therefore makes sense to talk about reconstructing the "market system" and figuring out ways to democratize it. It makes sense to think about Congress setting out general plans for energy conservation and health care, and to develop separate agencies to carry out these plans. The models here are the Social Security Administration and the Environmental Protection Agency. Only right wingers live in dread of such agencies, which could serve people even better if they were backed by higher budgets and an egalitarian majority in Congress.

Jeez, no third parties, no hope for a centrally planned economy, or even for market socialism. Are you sure you really are a consultant for egalitarian activists? And what about the many social movements that have worked so hard and gained so much? Where do they fit in?

4

SOCIAL MOVEMENTS
AND STRATEGIC NONVIOLENCE

So far this book has not suggested much more in principle than what reasonable American liberals might advocate. After all, working inside the Democratic Party and making use of the market are their bread and butter. True, they wouldn't like the idea of challenging elected mainstream liberals in primaries, as egalitarian activists have to do sooner or later if they are going to take over the party. Nor would they look forward to government-owned enterprises competing with private corporations, but overall they'd be only mildly discomfited by what has been said so far.

It is the next step that returns the overall program to ground more familiar to egalitarian activists: the need for nonelectoral social movements as the basis for making electoral politics and planning through the market more visible, popular, and useful. Egalitarian activists have been distinctive in their willingness to go to the streets to win people to their causes and create the political pressures necessary for the social changes they advocate. No important advance has been made without such an effort, and each movement has been able to invent new methods of strategic nonviolence appropriate to the particular time and circumstances.

Thus, egalitarian activists intuitively know what the social psychologists who study social movements also stress: There has to be a nonroutine dimension to any movement for change. It doesn't make any sense to people to say that things are terrible, so they should vote and write letters to their elected representatives. If things are going to change, then people have to get out of their routines one way or another. There has to be social disruption. There has to be a "getting in the way of power," as one author-activist puts it. There has to be a social movement that has a shared political identity.

This social disruption has to be created through the principled use of strategic nonviolence. Nonviolence is often thought of as a philosophy, a religious sentiment, or a moral renunciation of violence, or even as a way to create win-win situations for all concerned if there is enough love and understanding. Sometimes it is reduced to carefully orchestrated acts of civil disobedience in which the time and place of arrest have been negoti-ated beforehand with the police. However, it is in actual practice a strategy for winning in conflicts where there are real differences between the adver-saries, including class antagonisms. As a form of conflict, nonviolent direct action is best understood in terms of the same basic concepts that are used to understand violent (military) conflicts, because the underlying reality in both cases is the engagement in conflict over opposing perspectives and interests. Thus the phrase "strategic nonviolence," which is in fact what trade union organizers practice through strikes and what civil rights leaders employed through sit-ins, freedom rides, and boycotts. It is a form of strug-gle that is focused on prevailing despite the fact that the opponents—usually a government or power elite—have superior resources and are likely to use one or another form of violence if they think it can succeed.

Although nonviolence is a strategic choice, it has to be employed within the context of a larger and more encompassing value system for two crucial reasons. First, such a value system is necessary in order to deal with the most important problem in using strategic nonviolence: helping members refrain from violence in the face of delays, provocations, and violent acts by the opponents. The individual urge to retaliate violently to violent oppo-nents is difficult to resist, but any use of violence by the insurgents leads to the loss of moral credibility, repels potential allies, and seemingly justifies violent reprisals by the government. Second, the practice of strategic nonvi-olence has to be encased within a value system so that the opponents slowly can become convinced that the challengers will not suddenly resort to vio-lence when they think it will be to their advantage. American egalitarians need to demonstrate that their strong moral convictions are always going to be expressed in a way that is consistent with their deep belief in the dignity and rights of each person. A sudden shift to property destruction or armed struggle is not an option. Strategic nonviolence therefore takes training, great personal courage, and self-discipline.

Moreover, the sustained use of strategic nonviolence requires a sense of collective political identity based on shared programs and goals. Strategic nonviolence is the commitment of a collectivity that is out to win against great odds. Physical attacks on individuals or property destruction are therefore a violation of the movement's shared identity and of the values its members care about the most. Any resort to violence breaks down group cohesion as well as alienating the silent majority that has to be defined as eventual allies in the struggle.

For the civil rights movement, this normative sense and necessary value system were provided first of all by the deep religious faith of the key participants. Strategic nonviolence was practiced within the context of the African American Christian churches, with their deeply moving spirituals like "We Shall Overcome," and it was taught in black schools of theology. However, strategic nonviolence in the civil rights movement was also based in a strong belief in American democracy, a belief that was surprising to outsiders because of the despicable way in which African Americans have been treated throughout American history. Given the overwhelming violence that southern whites could employ with impunity, African Americans in the South of course fully understood that nonviolence was their only choice as a strategy, but it was their faith in Christianity and democracy that made their chosen strategy possible and sustainable.

For current-day egalitarians, a commitment to the freedoms and democratic procedures won by past egalitarians can provide the primary foundation for the practice of nonviolence, although some of them also draw on their religious values as well. This democratic commitment has the added virtue of narrowing the gap between egalitarians and mainstream liberals. In addition, a nonviolence orientation can be sustained by the knowledge that it helps to keep the egalitarian movement itself more democratic; it ensures that violence-prone dominators will not take over the movement and subvert its democratic aims. As many historical cases suggest, the most violent people soon rise to the top once the possibility of violence is introduced, and they often use their loyal followers to intimidate or kill rivals.

It may be arguable if it is claimed that there are no circumstances anywhere in the world where violent means can be justified by the peaceful and democratic goals of the instigators. It is hard to imagine that strategic nonviolence would work for slaves, Jews in Nazi Germany, or critics in Saddam Hussein's Iraq. Dictatorships of any kind usually only fall when there are disagreements among those at or near the top, or if external challenges to the power structure give the oppressed some new openings. There are few instances where dictatorships have been overcome internally by the oppressed majority.

But given the freedoms, civil liberties, and voting rights achieved by a long line of American egalitarians and liberals, there is no end that could be justified by violence, property destruction, or armed struggle in this country. Such actions undercut the democratic rights won by past egalitarians and play into the hands of the government, which has the power to isolate and defeat any violent movement. Furthermore, property destruction and armed struggle of any kind are overwhelmingly rejected by the vast majority of the American people. Due to their appreciation of the freedoms they do enjoy, and despite the economic unfairness they recognize and experience, average Americans are repelled by violent political acts, whether by right wingers or left wingers. If the goal is to build a larger movement that connects to a strategy to take over and transform the Democratic Party, not just to force the authorities to react to one or another provocation with slight reforms, then violence makes no sense. It is therefore both immoral and counterproductive for American egalitarians to employ violent strategies. Or, as Cesar Chavez used to say about violence when he was leading the farm workers' movement, it's wrong and it's stupid.

Violence-prone activists sometimes like to claim they are merely retaliating against violence by the police, which they think people will understand and even applaud as justifiable self-protection. Some activists also believe that standing up to the police will inspire others to join them because they have shown they are serious about challenging the system. However, as polls taken after such incidents show, most people do not accept these rationales. They do not like to hear of extreme reactions by the police, but they tend to blame the demonstrators, even when the police are the primary instigators. Thus, it is not a matter of who is right and who is wrong about which side started it. It is a matter of whether physical confrontations are effective in gaining adherents, and it seems clear that they are not.

To be effective, nonviolence must be maintained in the face of great provocations, even including beatings and murders by the opponents. If there is no retaliation, the perpetrators may be prosecuted, or public sentiment may switch to the side of the challengers. This is in fact in part what happened when police and vigilantes attacked civil rights demonstrators in the 1960s. Those unprovoked actions swung whites outside the South against police violence despite their continuing feelings of racial superiority, and forced the president and leaders in Congress to condemn elected officials and law enforcement personnel in the South.

Once nonviolence is taken seriously as the only and ideal strategy for egalitarians in a democratic society, it quickly leads to new ways of thinking about issues of social change. Creative tactics are often forthcoming when the seemingly simple and direct strategy of violence no longer crowds out the need for new ideas. Such issues as the following become central:

- What should be done to create the best possible environment for the use of strategic nonviolence?
- What can be done to win over those who are more or less neutral bystanders ("third parties")?
- What can be done to divide the opposition?
- What can be done to undermine the legitimacy of corporate and governmental opponents?
- What can be done to make repressive forces such as the police feel safe in the face of the demonstrators and perhaps less reliable for the opponents?

Within this context, the key issue for strategic nonviolent activists in a stable democratic country like the United States is to create and use tactics that cause the unexpected disruption of everyday life in ways that force people out of their routines, hurt the bottom line of businesses, or injure the electoral chances of politicians, while at the same time winning positive attention from the media. There is no one formula for how this is done; it is the product of activists whose experience and sense of timing lead to the right mix of tactics for the moment. Advocates of nonviolence have catalogued many such tactics, and they stress that new tactics are always being invented by new movements facing unique situations.

The successful tactics of the civil rights movement are well known through dozens of books and stunning documentaries like *Eyes on the Prize,* but they are always worth recalling as evidence for what strategic nonviolence can accomplish in the hands of a value-based movement with clear objectives. Each of its victories is a textbook example of how nonviolent tactics can create the necessary form of social disruption to force authorities to change specific unjust customs and laws. Bus boycotts, for example, caused financial crises for municipal bus systems and put white drivers out of work. Downtown boycotts and marches in many southern cities kept African American dollars out of the coffers of white merchants and scared away white shoppers, forcing business leaders and politicians to negotiate changes.

Sit-ins jolted people out of their routines, caused managers to close lunch counters to avoid serving African Americans, filled overcrowded jails, and exhausted the limited resources of local police forces. Freedom rides upset racist whites who enjoyed exercising their small rituals of racial superiority. The ensuing white violence forced the federal government to intervene on the side of the freedom riders, who soon included many northern whites drawn into the struggle by the courage and determination of the nonviolent activists. Giant marches to state capitals did not merely register the size and resolve of movement support, which is the main thing most current-day marches accomplish, but forced the police to protect African Americans from violent white racists.

Thanks to demonstrations in northern cities controlled by Democrats, and events like the March on Washington in 1963, the movement was able to disrupt the normal routines of the national-level Democratic Party. It drove a bigger wedge between northern and southern Democrats, forcing machine Democrats to choose between their public image as liberals and their backroom power deals with southern Democrats.

The gay and lesbian movement is the best recent example of how new and powerful tactics arise unexpectedly in the context of a movement. "Coming out" and "outing" may not seem like strategic nonviolence at first glance, but they can be seen in hindsight as the ideal nonviolent tactics to deal with the problems facing a group that is small in number—less than 3 percent of the population—and widely distributed by class, race, and gender. Coming out succeeds because it breaks the taboos that keep gays and lesbians closeted, and because it forces family members, friends, classmates, teammates, and coworkers to face the fact that their prejudices are affecting people close to them, not just an abstract group called "homosexuals" that is readily demonized due to cultural and religious traditions. Coming out also destroys stereotypes about gays and lesbians by showing they are successful as lawyers, doctors, business executives, and scholars.

It personalizes the issue in just the right way when the sister of a right-wing ideologue like Newt Gingrich announced that she is a lesbian and went on the campaign circuit, in effect dogging her brother wherever he went. It restrains an extreme rightist like Vice President Richard Cheney when his campaign has to deal with the fact that his daughter is an out lesbian, albeit one who shilled for corporations. Coming out also emboldened the most hesitant of gays, gay Republicans, to form their own club within the party in the late 1970s. These Log Cabin Republicans had five thousand members in fourteen states by the early 1990s.

But it is outing that may put the final nail in the coffin as far as the Republican use of homophobia to attract middle-income fundamentalist Christian voters. It is effective because it has an element of surprise, forces people out of their routine thought patterns, draws media attention, generates sympathy by exposing hypocrisy, and discredits those corporate-conservative political operatives who use homophobia to further the Republican Party even while being homosexuals themselves. Moreover, it did not take many outings for the fear of being outed to have a strong effect on the statements and votes of right-wing gays and lesbians. The tactic was first used in Washington with the outing of Pete Williams, the spokesperson for the Department of Defense in George H. W. Bush's administration. Williams, who became a familiar face on television due to the Persian Gulf War, was outed because gay activists were frustrated by the Republican resistance to facing the AIDS epidemic. They were also tired of seeing the Pentagon discharge gay and lesbian military personnel when most of the brass, and many other people in Washington, knew that Williams was gay. This exposure of gross hypocrisy left the Bush administration in a difficult position. Extreme rightists might be upset if he did not fire Williams, but Bush would look very bad to moderate voters if he summarily fired an otherwise acceptable Republican for his sexual orientation. Williams stayed.

When the right-wing chauvinist Patrick Buchanan gave his infamous speech about a new "culture war" to the 1992 Republican National Convention, in which he signaled that gays and lesbians would replace communists as the new hate/fear object for the right, it led to further outings and a large increase in the Log Cabin Republican membership. The gay male who wrote Bush's acceptance speech for the convention was outed, along with a Louisiana Republican in the House who often supported the opponents of gay and lesbian rights. Gay activists also delivered a stern lesson in 1996 when they outed a Republican congressman from Arizona via e-mail messages after he voted to deny federal recognition of same-sex marriages. He survived in the electoral arena and went on to give one of the addresses at the Republican National Convention in 2000, suggesting that the Republicans may be getting the message.

Much of the coming out and outing of the late 1980s and early 1990s was due to a new organization that used many forms of nonviolent direct action to create the necessary atmosphere of crisis for dealing with the AIDS epidemic. The AIDS Coalition to Unleash Power (ACT UP) was soon described as rude, rash, and effective as it disrupted staid governmental, research, and cultural meetings, often causing unpleasant confrontations that went too far for some members of the gay and lesbian movement. It also closed down a street in the Wall Street area for several hours over drug costs, put a giant condom over Senator Jesse Helms's home in North Carolina to protest his opposition to funds for AIDS prevention, and threw the ashes of AIDS victims on the lawn of the White House. However, it never went over the line as far as physical violence or property destruction, and it adjusted and adapted its strategies to suit the new conditions it helped create.

Despite the effectiveness of strategic nonviolence, complete adherence to it has been abandoned by some of the most visible and influential activists since the mid-1960s. This move toward the inclusion of violent acts in the repertoire of movement tactics began when Black Power advocates became increasingly impatient with the lack of responsiveness to plans for increasing political and economic integration after the civil rights movement achieved its primary goals through the Civil Rights Act of 1964 and the Voting Rights Act of 1965. They were first deeply disappointed by the failure of the 1964 Democratic National Convention to seat the integrated delegation of the Mississippi Freedom Democratic Party. That delegation was rejected, at the insistence of President Lyndon B. Johnson, except for two tokens, in favor of a racist delegation of traditional southern Democrats who would not even pledge to support the Democratic nominee. It was truly a defining moment, a great divide between egalitarians and liberals within the Democratic Party on how to confront southern white racists.

Militant black activists also watched in despair as the conservative voting bloc continued to limit those kinds of government spending that might give African Americans a chance to improve their economic position. Moreover, there was foot dragging and outright refusal by trade unions to integrate their apprenticeship programs. This situation suggested that the unionized white working class was not prepared to share good jobs with African Americans, belying the support for civil rights by many union leaders. Nor was there any sign of a loosening in residential segregation, which meant among other things that African Americans would not have access to the best public schools.

For understandable but lamentable reasons, then, several top leaders in the Student Nonviolent Coordinating Committee (SNCC) gave up on nonviolence and working with whites, creating conflict within the organization with those who wanted to continue as a nonviolent and integrated movement. Soon after, Black Power advocates won out in this argument, turning to inflammatory rhetoric about "taking up the gun" that threatened many whites and validated their worst fears. They then found allies in the North with the creation of the Black Panther Party, a self-identified revolutionary Marxist group whose goals and armed confrontations with the police led to shoot outs and deaths in several cities. The Black Power stance of the Black Panthers and what remained of SNCC gave the movement for African American equality and opportunity a violent and frightening new image that alienated most whites.

Feeling blocked on all sides, and doubting that whites would become any less prejudiced, many African American communities exploded on their own, starting in Harlem and Philadelphia in 1964, often in response to policy brutality, and with little or no prompting from Black Power advocates. These upheavals reached a peak in the extensive protests and property destruction in reaction to the assassination of Martin Luther King Jr. in 1968. Contrary to claims that they were aimless riots, they turned out to be more purposeful and targeted at specific businesses than was originally thought. Furthermore, there is reason to believe that jobs were created in response to these eruptions and funding for existing government programs directed at ghetto areas was increased. In the first few years after these long hot summers, it seemed like the uprisings had a payoff and therefore made some political sense.

However, with the help of hindsight a bigger fact needs to be faced: The long-term effects of the violence were negative. The outbursts were an understandable reaction to pent-up frustration and anger, and they had specific messages to deliver, but they were nonetheless a political mistake. The fact that they occurred shows the need for any future egalitarian movement to have its principles clear and in place before becoming involved in highly emotional events that are not easily understood or controlled as they unfold. It is not possible to spread the word about why violent disorders are not a good idea while they are happening. A new egalitarian movement would have to explain why they are unproductive well before they are on the horizon, not sit back and let them happen.

For example, the gulf between blacks and whites expanded as the disruptions continued over several summers. Suspicion and anger were increased on both sides. Cities like Newark and Detroit still had not recovered from the withdrawal of investment thirty-five years later. "Law and order" became a code word for the enlargement of a criminal justice system that was used to control black communities. White voters in the North expressed their approval of a hard-line government approach by voting against the Democratic candidates for president in 1968 and 1972, thereby helping to destroy the New Deal coalition in the process.

Polls are also quite telling on the negative consequences of violence. While American public opinion gradually liberalized from the 1960s to the 1980s on a wide range of issues championed by egalitarian movements, such as women's rights, it went the other way on anything to do with violence and disorder. For example, from 1965 to 1969 there was a 26 percent rise in the percentage of people saying that courts were not harsh enough, bringing the total to 83 percent. Support for the death penalty declined from 73 percent in 1953 to 47 percent in 1965, but then jumped back up to 50 percent in 1966 and to 80 percent by 1980.

Some of the college-based New Leftists in Students for a Democratic Society (SDS), originally inspired by the civil rights movement, also lost patience and turned to violent social disruption when they became antiwar activists. In this case, several key leaders began to talk about revolution and the possible use of violence well before antiwar frustration reached a high pitch in 1967 and 1968. In their anger and self-isolation from mainstream America, many of them seriously thought that a revolution might well occur. A small number, including some of the most visible and influential leaders, withdrew into "families" and cells, learned to shoot guns, and practiced self-defense for possible hand-to-hand combat. The tragedy is that they were being more effective as nonviolent activists than they realized. They had put the government on the defensive, as secret documents from the time now reveal, and mainstream people were slowly changing their minds on the war. Then the combination of Vietcong success in key battles and American students' protest at home led top American leaders to draw back in early 1968, just as the antiwar movement was talking openly about the alleged need for violence and taking more and more violent actions.

Despite their considerable accomplishments in leading the early antiwar movement, and their original distancing from Marxism, by 1969 all of the factions in SDS considered themselves revolutionary Marxists of one variety or another. But the increasingly fragmented movement had less success for the next several years, as seen by the fact that the war dragged on until 1975, and despite a new outpouring of liberal antiwar protest due to the American invasion of Cambodia in 1970. The antiwar movement suffered this decline because violence made the movement itself the issue. Its opponent could portray it as an attack on American values and the American government, thereby making it harder for the movement to gain new adherents. For example, these actions deeply alienated many white American workers, who stated their feelings by putting American flags on their hard hats. Most trade union leaders remained steadfast in their support of the war and criticized the student-based movement. With each antiwar bombing attack on university buildings and government facilities, which caused one death and several injuries, more and more students drew away from the antiwar leftists as well.

The emergence of violent actions also has limited the potential of the best-known nonelectoral effort of recent years: the global justice movement that burst into public consciousness due to its opposition to the World Trade Organization (WTO). The first American anti-WTO gathering, in conjunction with the WTO meeting in Seattle in 1999, was impressive for the size of the turnout—forty to fifty thousand—and the breadth of the coalition, including union members and environmentalists. It had the virtue of warning multinational corporations and government officials that they would face a backlash in their drive to globalization if they did not change their tune on a wide range of issues. It helped create a context in which the Third World countries could reject the terms the developed countries were offering them at that meeting, although their concerns on environmental and labor issues were more nearly the opposite to those of the demonstrators. As a result of these efforts, the globalizers have expressed their concerns about the issues they previously ignored and tried to initiate a dialogue with at least some organizations in the global justice movement.

The left press celebrated the large turnout and the failure of the meetings to lead to a new trade agreement as heralding a revival of the left, but the "Battle of Seattle" was actually the beginning of another end, because the nonviolent groups were not able to control the trashing of stores and the battles with police by many dozens of property-destruction activists at the height of the demonstrations. Earlier in the year, many of these same people had used sledgehammers and crowbars to attack restaurants and stores in Eugene, Oregon. They had also posted messages on the Internet and distributed leaflets making known some of their intentions, so there was fair warning of what could happen. Indeed, many of the nonviolent activists thought they had negotiated an agreement that there would be no destruction of property, at least not on the same day that they were successfully denying access to buildings by means of nonviolent direction action.

Measured by the necessities of strategic nonviolence, it is not good enough to say that most groups involved in the anti-WTO demonstrations did not approve of violent actions, or that these actions were carried out by only a minute percentage of demonstrators. As always, the destructive acts became the main issue for many local citizens and bitterly divided those who participated in the marches and nonviolent direct actions, forcing them to takes sides in an argument over something they didn't think should have happened. Rather than condemning these actions as self-defeating, most of the left press downplayed the violence and simply emphasized that the overall demonstrations were successful in making their point. As the *Nation*'s correspondent put it,

> The media focus on a few broken store windows should not distract from the profundity of what has happened here. A phantasmagorical mix of tens of thousands of peaceful demonstrators—husky, red-jacketed steelworkers marching alongside costumed sea turtle impersonators, environmentalists with miners, human rights activists with small family farmers—stood against the WTO, succeeded in closing down its opening sessions and thrust the once-obscure issue of fair trade onto center stage.

However, the property destruction added up to at least a few hundred thousand dollars in damages and lost sales, and maybe a few million, although the exact amount is disputed. There was also much negative press, as is always the case for any kind of destruction or violence, whether political or not. In addition, the hopes for the new coalition that was supposed to grow out of this demonstration turned out to be in large part illusory. The dream of a Teamsters and turtles coalition soon faded as the Teamsters, the United Mine Workers, and some building trade unions curried favor with the Republicans and supported environmentally unsound government initiatives in the name of job creation. Other unions withdrew their support, too, partly because of the fallout from the violence, which was generally criticized by the twenty-five thousand union members taking part in the marches.

Moreover, the relatively minor property destruction and clashes with the police in Seattle were only the beginning because they were in good part the product of believers in a form of direct action that sees property destruction as a method of empowerment. The confrontations therefore escalated at the anti-WTO demonstration in Quebec City, Canada, in 2000, where some of the marchers left the route of the nonviolent march to throw rocks and bottles at the police, who were deployed behind a high-wire fence that was torn down by some demonstrators to create a direct confrontation. The next day the same demonstrators smashed windows in nearby stores, including the army-navy store where they purchased gas masks and other equipment for their attack on the fence.

A prodestruction leader named Howl, who trained students in these tactics at both Bard and Vassar, justified such attacks in an interview with the correspondent for *In These Times* by saying that the people she knew were impatient and wanted "action," not mere demonstrations. When asked about an anarchist text that argued for nonviolent direct action, she replied that "the statement bugs me because it makes a huge assumption about time. For most people [the social crisis is] really urgent and really immediate. I think that's the kind of attitude that turns off people of color and working-class folks, because of the perceived wishy-washy nature of anarchism. As much as some of us would like to process shit forever, we need to take action." This is a formulation that is sure to alienate the overwhelming majority of Americans, turning the movement into a permanent minority that will become increasingly isolated from other social movements and any form of electoral politics.

By the next year in Genoa, Italy, the anti-WTO demonstrations were essentially street battles, and a demonstrator was killed by the police when they felt they were under attack. Some of the property-destruction activists also suffered brutal beatings at the hands of the police. When fifty thousand members of the global justice movement met in São Paulo, Brazil, in January 2002, in the aftermath of this death, there were some second thoughts about the productiveness of violence, but by then it was too late. The same *Nation* correspondent who hoped the violence in Seattle would not be a distraction now stressed that the movement was at a low ebb once again due to the violence: "It would be disingenuous to deny that the U.S. movement faces serious roadblocks. The blue-green coalition has frayed, and tension between much of organized labor and the rest of the movement is real. 'The biggest problem inside the Seattle coalition isn't the [antiterrorist] war,' said one key U.S. activist. 'The problem is around those who want to use violence.'"

The correspondent also quotes a European environmentalist to make the same point: "Too often we get dragged into a swamp debating what is euphemistically called 'diversity of tactics.' Now we need to speak up and say clearly that violence, as a political tactic, just doesn't work either in the United States or in Europe."

The shocking terrorist attacks on September 11, 2001, coming just six weeks after Genoa, add to the likelihood that any type of property destruction or confrontation with police at future anti-WTO demonstrations would be highly counterproductive. They would anger the overwhelming majority of Americans and meet with strong repression on the part of the government. Reassessment therefore becomes a necessity, providing an opportunity for a new start based on the realization that the property destruction and physical attacks on the police of the previous few years led the movement into a dead end. When demonstrations emerge once again, they should be based on a commitment to the strategic, nonviolent forms of direct action advocated throughout this chapter. Such a commitment leaves plenty of room to disrupt routines and get in the way of power without dividing the movement and alienating potential supporters, and it is far more effective in the long run. This commitment should include the principles put forth by advocates of strategic nonviolence for dealing with proviolence groups. Nonviolent groups should distance themselves from violent groups and strongly condemn their philosophies and actions. Only groups that specifically state that they are completely committed to strategic nonviolence should be allowed to be cosponsors of marches and participate in their planning.

Take over the Democratic Party. Advocate extensive economic planning through a reconstructed market system that aims for greater equality, worker rights, and environmental protection. Practice strategic nonviolence in a creative fashion when the time is ripe with the goal of winning over neutrals, dividing the opposition, discrediting government authorities, and reassuring police officers about their personal safety. No one of these points is earthshaking. Taken together, however, they are a new package that has never been tried. They unite the electoral and nonelectoral. They bypass the structural impossibilities of third parties and central planning, and they eliminate the self-defeating resort to violence. They are the central pieces that make it possible for a new egalitarian movement to create alliances with mainstream liberals and work with elected liberal politicians on some issues. But still more is needed.

5

REDEFINING WHO'S US
AND WHO'S THEM

There is a standard story line for insurgent social movements of both the left and right that goes something like this: The country is sustained by good and hardworking average people in the middle like us, but we have little or no power. For the left, these good people are the workers, for the right they are the middle class of small business owners, farmers, and white-collar workers. However, these good people are exploited and dominated by the few at the top, who are the capitalists for the leftists and the bureaucrats, internationalist financiers, and atheists for the right. Moreover, the good people have to contend with the ne'er-do-wells or lackeys of the rich, who are called the "lumpen proletariat" and "petite bourgeoisie" by the leftists and the welfare bums and shiftless people of color by the right.

Since this state of affairs is not fair to the good and hardworking majority, they have a right to be angry, and they should organize to create social change that brings about a new social order, which is a transition to socialism, gender equality, and racial equality for the left, and a return to an idyllic world of small business, small government, male dominance, and white Christian rule for the right.

Social science research supports part of this picture through studies of social stratification and the wealth distribution. There is indeed an obvious pecking order from top to bottom in terms of jobs, education, and social status, although the reasons why some people end up on the bottom are far different from what the political right imagines. It is also well documented that the few at the top have a highly disproportionate share of wealth and income. In 1998, the last year for which figures from the Federal Reserve Board are available, the top 1 percent owned 47.3 percent of "financial wealth," defined as marketable assets minus the value of owner-occupied housing. This small sliver has two-thirds of the business equity, half of the stock and trust equity, and one-third of investment real estate.

If the upper 10 percent is considered, it has 90 percent of the stock, bonds, trusts, and business equity, and about 75 percent of nonhome real estate. That doesn't leave much for the bottom 90 percent. Wealth has not been this concentrated since 1929. Figures on inheritance paint the same stark picture: 91.9 percent receive nothing. Only 1.6 percent receive $100,000 or more, and another 1.1 percent receive $50,000 to $100,000. When it comes to income, the percentage received by the highest 1 percent has increased to 16.6 percent, up from 12.8 percent in 1982. The top 10 percent receives 41.4 percent, up from 32 percent in the early 1980s. All that most Americans have is a paycheck, a house with a mortgage, and personal belongings. What working Americans can give their children is access to education and maybe some job contacts.

The salaries of chief corporate executives have grown at a rate of about 6 percent per year since the 1980s. The highest 1 percent have captured a stunning 94 percent of the increase in total income since 1973. American chief executives make four times as much as their counterparts in Germany and France. They make twenty-four times as much as the average production worker, whereas in Germany chief executives only make eight times as much. These numbers cannot be explained by "market forces." They show the importance of political power, with "market forces" used as the cover story. More and more, it is corporate executives, not just rich stockholders, who rule America. They are the leadership core of the corporate-conservative coalition.

Thus, there's good reason to believe that the top 1 percent of wealth holders form a capitalist class and have a dominant role in the economy and government. They can invest where and when they wish to, move offices and factories at a moment's notice, and hire and fire most workers at will. They have a monopoly of policy expertise through thousands of charitable foundations, an array of think tanks, and several policy discussion groups where the experts tell busy corporate leaders what their options are. They have a huge number of lobbyists and public relations people. They can have a big impact on politicians through campaign donations, and they can offer cushy jobs to well-behaved politicians after they retire or lose an election. They get themselves appointed to top positions in Washington.

However, this picture of economic concentration and class domination doesn't mean that it makes good political sense to frame the conflict primarily in terms of one social class against another in trying to bring about egalitarian social change. That's a surprising statement, I realize, but defining the "opponents" as "the capitalists" or "the rich" is a strategic mistake for several reasons that are spelled out in this chapter. If the problem is developing new policies and gaining political power, which it is, then the struggle should be framed from the start as a political one, not an economic one. The in-group should be all those who come to embrace the program of the egalitarian movement, and the out-group should be all those who oppose such changes. If the conflict is framed in this way, an egalitarian coalition has a chance to win over the moderates, neutrals, and independents who currently identify with capitalists and who might be offended by blanket criticisms of them as a class. It may even attract dissident members of the capitalist class who transcend their class interests and in the process become very valuable in legitimating the movement to those in the middle who are hesitant to climb on board.

But a class framing is not just a problem in terms of labeling all capitalists as enemies. Once the conflict is framed in class terms, those defined as members of the working class take on all virtue, and those outside the working class are ignored or demonized, whether they are rich or not. In fact, it is very difficult to decide who is in the working class and who is not, which leads to further problems for the movement. For example, the leading American Marxists of the 1870s, most of them German American immigrants with a European perspective, defined the working class narrowly in terms of trade unionists, all of whom happened to be white and male. This meant that the many women and African American activists of the day were ignored or opposed by them. American-born skilled craftsmen, viewed as mere reformers, were also excluded.

One hundred years later, many of the new revolutionary Marxist activists on college campuses decided that their main focus had to be workers in blue-collar jobs, preferably in unions, although this time people of color and women were as important as white males. Everyone else below the capitalist class was dismissed as petite bourgeoisie, meaning people who were believed to be potential right wingers, a demonization that almost guaranteed that they would become enemies of the left whether they started out that way or not. These activists took jobs in factories, joined the

Teamsters, and tried to convert blue-collar workers to a socialist perspective, with little or no success. Meanwhile, there were fewer and fewer blue-collar workers and a declining number of workers in unions.

Doing politics in terms of class categories also does not make sense because it does not sit well with most of the everyday working people to whom it is meant to appeal. The whole thrust of the average Americans' experience is to break down class distinctions, not heighten them. They do not like to think of themselves in terms of their class identity, which immediately reminds them that they are not rich and have a lower status than they might like. True, Americans are mostly talking about what sociologists call "status groups" when they discuss class, but social classes as Americans understand them have much overlap with their economic standing, and trying to make the distinction between "status group" and "class" in a political context doesn't seem to have much chance.

Americans never have liked the idea of class, period, and this is not simply a denial of reality or the product of ideological hype. It is a matter of what social identities people prefer to emphasize, which in the United States have not included class for a variety of historical reasons. Most Americans below the wealthy and professional classes understand that they have differing interests from the upper levels when it comes to wages, working conditions, taxes, and government benefits. Poll after poll shows that they would like to see their own interests realized, but not by defining one class against the other. It therefore makes no psychological or political sense to try to impose a class identity on people just because there's a social structure out there or some theory says it's a good idea to do politics in class terms.

In addition, a class framing is problematic because many egalitarians who agitate for social change do not come from the working class, however broadly it is defined, which makes them look like they are practicing a form of noblesse oblige. They often come from professional or wealthy families, obtain good educational credentials, and find work in or around university settings. Rather than claiming that they speak in the name of the working class, which rings hollow with most blue-collar and white-collar workers, they should put forth a program based on planning through the market that alters the class structure and then try to develop a value-based coalition that includes everyone willing to support it. This coalition might include some people of wealth who support greater equality for a variety of reasons, including religious values or ethnic background, but their inclusion is not encouraged when the conflict is stated in class terms.

The ideal model for a more open-ended framing of a social conflict is provided by the civil rights movement, which refused to define "whites" as the enemy, but only "racists" and "bigots." Racists and bigots included most whites in the South at that time, of course, so there was a clear opposition out there, but at the same time there was room for prointegration whites. Drawing on the Christian tradition, the movement therefore was able to utilize the concepts of forgiveness, redemption, and conversion in the service of strategic nonviolence to forge a black–white coalition. By opening its doors to people who believed in equal rights for African Americans whatever their class, race, religion, or previous beliefs, the movement was able to use these concepts to make it permissible for people to change their attitudes without violating their self-images as decent people ("saving face"). This strategy also had great appeal because it made sense to the many "third parties"—bystanders and observers—outside the South who were witnesses to the struggle. In similar fashion, if a "cross-class" coalition is going to be necessary to assemble a majority for an egalitarian program in the twenty-first century, then it is better to begin with a political framing of the us-versus-them issue that does not define one class or another as the enemy.

This approach to social change receives strong support from a long tradition of experimental studies of in-groups and out-groups in social psychology. First, studies of in-groups and out-groups show how readily people create such categories, even when the basis for distinctions are few and minor, probably because being part of an in-group reduces social uncertainty, enhances self-esteem, and satisfies psychological needs for a sense of belonging and identity. Such studies also reveal how quickly people invest strong emotional energy in the categories, feeling positive toward those they define as in their group and, with the right kind of encouragement, highly negative toward those in the out-group. It is clearly quite easy to become extremely antagonistic toward opponents due to this form of thinking, which is why who is us and who is them has to be defined very carefully from the start.

At the same time, experimental studies by social psychologists show that an us-versus-them framing is a powerful basis for a social movement. An in-group definition provides a strong sense of solidarity. It makes possible social comparisons with privileged exclusionary groups, which can generate a sense of injustice and contribute to a willingness to act. The problem, then, is to define the out-group in such a way that it is possible for people to abandon this group and join the in-group. Thus, the out-group should not be defined by characteristics that it cannot relinquish, such as gender, race, ethnicity, sexual orientation, or class origins. So, how should the conflict over transforming American society be framed by nonviolent egalitarian activists?

Given the changing social composition of the Democratic Party, and the need to avoid a class framing of the in-group and the out-group, it is the "corporate-conservative coalition" and the Republican Party that should be the designated opponents of the egalitarian activists. Indeed, they are the most clear, vocal, and organized opposition to any form of progressive social change, as evidenced by their economic and social policies since at least the 1970s. Framing the general conflict in terms of egalitarians versus corporate conservatives, and of Democrats versus Republicans in the political arena, has two distinct advantages in addition to avoiding a demonization of "the rich" or the capitalist class. First, these are categories from which people can remove themselves. They can change their minds and become Democrats, as many former Republicans in the Northeast already have done over the past thirty-five years.

Second, these categories leave a great many people as "third parties" who do not feel labeled as enemies and put on the defensive by criticisms of the corporate-conservative coalition and the Republican Party. In polls taken in 2001, only 31 percent of the respondents identified themselves as Republicans, with 22 percent saying they are independents and 36 percent saying they are Democrats. At the same time, 36 percent said they are conservatives, 40 percent said they are moderates, and 19 percent said they are liberals. Thus, a focus on the corporate-conservative coalition and the Republicans as the opposition leaves egalitarians with a potential majority of liberals, moderates, independents, and Democrats to win to their side.

But who is the egalitarian "we" who do battle with the corporate-conservative coalition if it is not "the working class"? It starts with the multiple *wes* who currently make up the nonviolent insurgent groups in the United States, the coalition of white progressives, liberal people of color, progressive trade unionists, feminists, living-wage activists, environmentalists, gay and lesbian activists, global justice activists, and antisweatshop activists who work together on many issues and often vote for one or another Democrat in partisan elections. From there the coalition has to build out to the neutrals, bystanders, moderates, and skeptics who are the majority at the present time. Within this context, the movement has to offer everyone a shared common political identity that does not attempt to downplay or erase their current social identities. And that is where the concept of "egalitarian" comes into the picture once again. Egalitarianism is not only a set of values that a great many Americans endorse in the abstract, but it can provide the basis for a collective social identity within the political arena for a coalition-based movement.

Once a framing in terms of egalitarian Democrats versus corporate conservatives and Republicans is in place, then it is possible for "the social system" to become reattached to the actual individuals who run it without danger of losing focus or making enemies out of potential allies. First and foremost, the chief executive officers of major corporations become fair game because they call the shots for the corporate-conservative coalition and regularly oppose egalitarian policy proposals. So, too, should a wide range of business organizations be named and criticized because they are on record with a set of policy recommendations that are not to the benefit of those in the egalitarian coalition. For example, the Business Roundtable and the U.S. Chamber of Commerce, which are just about command central for the corporate conservatives, are completely wrong from an egalitarian viewpoint about how the expansion of global trade should be structured, and therefore must be challenged through demonstrations, marches, media campaigns, and lobbying efforts. President George W. Bush is certainly open to criticism as the current political leader of the corporate-conservative coalition and as a defender of unfair trade, draconian welfare policies, and meager health care proposals.

For that matter, specific Democrats can be criticized within this overall context, such as members of the Democratic Leadership Council, because they still function as part of the corporate-conservative coalition. Senator Joseph Lieberman of Connecticut can be rightly called the senator from the insurance industry. He is also the person who fought hardest in the Senate in 1994 and 2002 to allow corporations to receive tax deductions for the outrageous stock options they grant to their executives as a way to give them extra millions each year. As for Albert Gore Jr., he caved in to the corporate-conservative coalition on so many environmental issues that he cannot be treated with kid gloves by environmentalists and should draw strong egalitarian opposition in Democratic primaries if he tries to run for president again.

But an attack on "the rich" or "the capitalist class," or worse, "the capitalist pigs and bloodsuckers"? Then what about George Soros, the billionaire who thinks markets mostly get things wrong and that government is needed to fix these wrongs? His substantial financial support for various egalitarian causes, including the movement for more humane drug policies, has been very important. And what about Senator Jon Corzine of New Jersey, the centimillionaire banker who has gone beyond his class interests to advocate a "sharply defined progressive agenda—one that is committed to fighting for practical and progressive policies for working families and America's middle class—even when that means challenging powerful interests and the status quo"? He opposed Bush's tax cuts for the rich, wants an "activist" government, sees a universal health care system as a "basic right," and opposes the death penalty.

Combined with programs for planning through the market, full employment, and an expansion of the earned income tax credit, the Corzine program would be a giant step forward in improving the day-to-day lives of the 80 percent of Americans who have benefited little or not at all from the growth of the economy since the 1980s. Is there an egalitarian in America who would hesitate for one second in accepting this package as a great start after decades of Richard M. Nixon, Gerald R. Ford, Jimmy Carter, Ronald Reagan, George H. W. Bush, Bill Clinton, and George W. Bush?

Shouldn't Corzine, a straight white male centimillionaire, with a wife who is a strong feminist, be in the coalition? Is he one of "us" or one of "them"?

6

KEEPING LEADERS ACCOUNTABLE

Courageous and farsighted leadership is as essential to an egalitarian social movement as any other collective human enterprise, but leaders can destroy the movement and undermine its goals in the process of building it if there are not mechanisms to hold them accountable from the start. This is once again the general problem of domination, the tendency for some people to think they are superior to others on some dimension or another and therefore are justified in excluding or dominating those who are deemed inferior. As noted in chapter 1, elitist thinking such as this is a tendency that can develop in any group or movement even though its natural home is on the right, and it can manifest itself as ethnic pride, racial superiority, gender dominance, and much else.

This problem is probably as old as the human species. There is now evidence that it may have been a persistent issue in the small hunting and gathering bands in which human beings lived for their first one hundred thousand or so years. Members of such bands shared meat with the group as a whole, which suggests a general cooperative tendency in human beings that transcends family ties. But sharing and cooperation may not be the whole story. Contrary to the image that members of these groups were naturally egalitarian, which leaves the emergence of later power structures as an ongoing puzzle, it now seems possible that they had "inverted power structures" in which the group as a whole was organized informally to control any headstrong individual or bully who attempted to become the dominant member of the group.

The rank and file exerted their control in these small bands of five hundred or so people through mundane but important mechanisms such as gossip, which alerted everyone to potential problems. Once an informal consensus was reached, the would-be power tripper was subjected to ridicule and the cold shoulder. If those didn't work, the band resorted to exclusion from intimate conversations, expulsion from the group, threats, or even assassination. The first egalitarians may have been a combative and cantankerous bunch.

The need for these various practices in small preliterate cultures suggests that there is a tendency to dominate, at least in some people, but also a desire not to be dominated, and hence the tug and pull between potential dominators and the inverted power structure. Ordinary people finally lost this battle five thousand years ago with the rise of civilization in a handful of separate places across the globe, but not without a struggle. The advent of civilizations meant that domination now had a stable organizational base in the increasingly specialized but intertwined economic, political, military, and religious realms. Leaders who could gain control of these types of organizations were difficult to dislodge. When a leadership group could combine economic, political, and military power, and then pass privileges along to its children, it became a "ruling class."

Since that long ago time, ruling classes have been the rule rather than the exception. Everyday people are usually divided among themselves and organizationally outflanked by their well-organized dominators, so they rarely have had any influence in very many places for very long. This nearly unbroken record of domination and subjugation is what makes the partial successes of democracy over the past three hundred years so valuable and worth preserving. Building on those accomplishments, it is modern-day egalitarians who have taken up the task of trying to create inverted power structures in highly developed industrialized civilizations.

However, the potential for domination by leaders remains a major problem even inside the egalitarian movements themselves. They, too, have a need for an inverted power structure if they are not to end up doing what they set out to undo. If anything, the need is all the greater because creating a new organization or climbing to a leadership role in an established organization can reinforce domination tendencies. It can also provide the new leader with the network of outside contacts, overall organizational understanding, and financial resources to gain complete control of the organization. Many years ago, a political scientist in Germany sadly concluded that "he who says organization says oligarchy." He formulated his pessimistic Iron Law of Oligarchy on the basis of his experience in the German Social Democratic Party, the largest and strongest socialist organization in Europe prior to World War I.

Consider the more recent case of Cesar Chavez, mentioned in chapter 4 as an advocate of nonviolence, who was an inspiring leader who gave organizers room to be creative and thereby built a multiethnic coalition of farm workers. His charisma was such that he also attracted many students and recent college graduates who worked for years to help the union for little or no pay. Starting out in the 1960s, he made slow but steady progress, convincing many liberal politicians and leaders in the Catholic Church to support the movement. Then, after a series of victories in the mid-1970s, and the election of a liberal Democratic governor who pushed for a California Farm Labor Board, it looked like the United Farm Workers were on the verge of major success. Contracts were signed with a few liberal growers, and some of the more conservative growers signaled that they might be willing to bargain after years of resistance.

But the union faltered badly between 1978 and 1983 for several reasons. It had to fight off an attempt by the Teamsters to move into parts of agriculture through arranging sweetheart contracts with growers. It also had to deal with a right-wing Republican governor elected in 1982, who appointed a vicious agribusiness lawyer as the head of the farm labor board. However, the story of the failure is much more complicated and tragic than most activists imagine. In fact, Chavez himself played the major role in undermining the union's victories because he could not delegate and share power. He could not abandon his all-powerful leadership role to create a normally functioning organization in which many people playing specialized roles had significant decision-making power. He could not resist giving the best jobs to his friends and relatives.

Long-time coworkers were forced to take part in a form of encounter group called the "Synonon Game," in which they were unmercifully criticized and browbeaten. They found themselves fired and ordered out of the union's compound in a small mountain town at a moment's notice, sleeping in their cars for a few days until they recovered from the shock. Loyal legal aides who were trying to negotiate contracts were accused of disloyalty and asked to resign. The bargaining team fell apart, and most of the growers took advantage of this opportunity to return to an oppositional stance. It was as if Chavez could not let the movement for which he labored so long become a bread-and-butter union with different departments dealing with different issues, including complicated contracts with growers. Today, the farm workers union is a mere shell of its former self, run by Chavez's hand-picked son-in-law.

As a left-wing expert on labor organizing who followed the whole history of the farm worker struggle once put it: "Cesar Chavez created the United Farm Workers and Cesar Chavez destroyed the United Farm Workers." Most egalitarians who know little about the union's history continue to believe otherwise, but until they can face and overcome terrible truths such as this, they will forever fail and continue to blame others for their failures.

Or recall the outcome when Jesse Jackson created the Rainbow Coalition and ran for president in the 1984 and 1988 primaries, claiming that he wanted to build an organization that could internally challenge the Democratic Party. It was the right idea and there was a good platform, but Jackson was the wrong person as far as creating an organization to transform the party. Thanks to his great charisma and eloquent speaking style, Jackson energized black voters, who used the opportunity of his candidacy to send the message that they wanted to have more power within the party. His overall vote total went from 18.5 percent in 1984 to 29.7 percent in 1988, with an improvement from 21 to 32 percent in Florida and from 10 to 38 percent in the very white state of Oregon.

Although his core vote was in the black community, Jackson won 30 percent of Hispanic votes and 12 percent of white votes in 1988. He may have received as many as 40 percent of the white vote in his upset victory in the Michigan caucuses in 1988. These vote totals are all the more impressive because he alienated many Democratic voters through his relationship with black Muslim leader Louis Farrakhan and his use of the term "hymie" to characterize Jews. Despite these and other mistakes, he won the fear and respect of Bill Clinton and Albert Gore Jr. in the 1988 primaries, thereby ensuring himself of White House visits and media attention during their administration.

But he did not really try to build a lasting political organization that could be the base for an egalitarian wing in the party, because his main goal was to control everything and keep himself in the spotlight. He fought for progressive causes, but he did not delegate, follow through, or tolerate the success of any other potential leaders. In the 1988 campaign, he drove away any notable person he saw as a possible rival and treated many members of his staff very badly, often scapegoating them for his own failures. His disappointed supporters drifted away and he used his Chicago-based civil rights organization, Rainbow/PUSH, to advance his personal agenda, frittering away whatever moral authority he had left. Jackson's campaigns once again suggest that working within the Democratic Party can have a real impact, but they also show the pitfalls of allowing an egotistical leader to control the campaign.

Lest these two accounts make the problem appear to be males, not organizational dynamics, it is instructive to look at the history of one of the more remarkable revolutionary Marxist groups of the 1970s, the Democratic Workers Party. It was distinguished from other such groups in two unique ways. It was led in good part by women, and it was not oriented toward the Soviet Union, China, or any other foreign revolution. Like the other revolutionary Marxist groups, however, it had few or no workers despite its name. In fact, it may have had the highest concentration of Ph.D.s, M.D.s, lawyers, and social workers of any political group in the country.

Despite its goals and the educational backgrounds of its most active members, it nonetheless became distinguished by the unchallenged power of its chair, Marlene Dixon, a former sociology professor. As she settled into her role and as her stature and self-importance grew, she became more and more outrageous and arbitrary. For example, Dixon had members doing her housecleaning and she maintained a luxurious lifestyle. She signed her name to articles and books written by others on topics about which she had little or no knowledge. There is also evidence that she used threats and intimidation to influence those who disagreed with her. Cars were spray painted, houses were ransacked, and the meetings of other leftist groups were disrupted.

After one or two years of intense work on party building, which expanded the group from a few dozen to several hundred, Dixon and her closest associates on the central committee suddenly expelled several of those who helped found the party for having the wrong views, and then insisted that none of the remaining members talk to them. Since party members often lived together in collectives, spent most of their time on party work, and had become close personal friends, this was a devastating penalty for differences of opinion. Most surprisingly, the members went along with the silence treatment, causing those who were expelled even greater personal isolation and anguish. After a ten-year effort that included community work, single-issue front organizations, and a third-party run for the governorship of California that received almost fifty thousand votes, the members confessed their great despair to each other and finally rejected Dixon, who was in any case talking about taking an elite few to Washington to start a leftist think tank.

Like the Chavez and Jackson examples, the case of the Democratic

Workers Party raises all the key problems of developing an egalitarian movement that does not succumb to the Iron Law of Oligarchy. Indeed, the party showed many of the characteristics that are typical of cult movements. As with cults, the members were normal people who wanted to be part of a project that would give more meaning to their lives. It was their willingness to sacrifice their personal lives for a cause they believed in that led them to endure the endless criticism that was part of being a member of the group. Many of them were somewhat younger than Dixon, which set her up as a respected adult figure. They admired her expertise and were proud to be part of the many study groups and research projects undertaken by the party. They felt part of an important in-group due to the secrecy with which the party operated, even to the point of adopting new "party" names that they used with each other. As with cults, Dixon only gradually realized as the organization developed that she could demand more and more of the members without encountering resistance. As in cults, the members slowly found themselves doing things they did not really want to do, but they went along anyhow because they thought everyone else was in agreement. Furthermore, by then they had no place to turn because they had few friends or contacts outside the group.

Some of these worrisome problems concerning the headstrong nature of egalitarian leaders may have been present in the Ralph Nader presidential campaign. As his book makes clear, he undertook the effort despite the fact that many of his closest activist associates refused to join him. He lists their names and has the nerve to chastise them for not living up to an earlier promise to support him if he ran for president. He then remarks: "When I reminded them of that previous assurance, they said what they meant was if I ever ran as a Democrat." He apparently did not stop to consider that he may be off base if his coworkers of such long standing disagreed with him about trying to start a third party.

Nor did Nader listen when those who did join him tried to give him advice about the dry and lengthy nature of many of his speeches. Instead, he lectured them on how important it is to provide basic lessons in civics until people get it right. For all the talk about building an organization, it was clearly a one-man show when Nader went on the road. By and large, he was surrounded by young people who wanted to be around him because of his shining reputation, but who were not in any position to give him honest feedback that he would accept.

Most troublesome of all, Nader may have kept his real motives from his followers. He may have been out to teach Gore a lesson for the disrespectful way he believed Gore had treated him in the previous few years. But that is not something he could say directly and win support from those who wanted to vote their consciences and stay clear of impure parties like the Democrats. He almost says as much in his book when he talks about the need for the Democrats to lose on occasion to keep them respectful of consumer and environmental activists. He certainly acted as if that was his real motive when he headed off to Miami to do last-minute campaigning in a state that everyone knew was too close to call, and in the face of the fact that some of his prominent supporters wanted him to demonstrate his clout by asking his supporters to vote for Gore in Florida.

Although Nader never publicly said that punishing Gore was his motive, that's the impression one disillusioned supporter received when he talked to a leader in the campaign about withdrawing from swing states like Florida, or asking Nader supporters in such states to hold their noses and vote for Gore in exchange for Nader votes by Democrats in safe states. The idea was that such a move would help defeat Bush while increasing the Nader vote in safe states. This would also vividly demonstrate the importance of Nader and his constituency to a Gore administration and Democrats everywhere, or so some of his supporters reasoned. In response to this suggestion, one of Nader's top aides abruptly said, "We are not going to do that." When the surprised supporter asked why not, the aide replied, "Because we want to punish the Democrats, we want to hurt them, wound them."

Thus far, few analysts have closely examined Nader's motives, but a staff writer for the *Philadelphia Inquirer* also reported that Nader wanted to punish Gore and the Democrats. After meeting with Nader in the spring of 2001, he wrote: "[Nader] is not coy about his motives. Just as he ran for president to punish Gore and the Democrats for allegedly betraying their progressive traditions and currying favor with global corporate power, now he wants to knock off congressional Democrats who have committed the same sins." The journalist is referring to Nader's plan to run sixty or so Greens in the congressional elections in 2002, which led to fewer candidates than originally anticipated and no successes.

Whatever Nader's actual motives, the point is that he has as many serious weaknesses as a leader as Chavez, Jackson, and the chair of the Democratic Workers Party. All four are unresponsive and dominating figures who drew their eager supporters into trying to build organizations that failed in their stated purpose. How, then, can an egalitarian movement avoid these kinds of negative outcomes while at the same time having spokespersons who represent and spread the collective sense of "we-ness" by outlining the program and criticizing the corporate-conservative coalition? First, at the level of individual organizations, there has to be (1) a set of organizational rules that are ratified by the founding members, (2) an elected leadership council, and (3) the ability to replace the top leader or leaders by a vote of the membership. This is the "constitutionalism" emphasized by liberals and often ignored to their own peril by egalitarians. It is a necessity that would also narrow the gap between egalitarians and liberals. Furthermore, people who do not want to work or campaign in the context of these rules would not join, which would eliminate some potential dominators.

Second, the movement has to be made up of a network of organizations, not one big organization. This makes it less likely that a few top leaders will take over everything. It also gives individual activists more freedom because they can register their dissatisfaction by leaving one organization and joining another. This freedom helps to keep organizational leaders more responsive. In addition, a network of organizations is the best way to accommodate the multiple social identities that inevitably will be present in a movement based on a coalition of groups. In a network of organizations, there would be no pressure to abandon current social identities in favor of an overriding one required by one big hierarchical organization.

To keep the general movement on the pathways suggested in preceding chapters, however, each organization would have to have the following three commitments built into its rules. Any organization that did not have these three commitments would not be invited to participate in events sponsored by organizations that accept the commitments. In effect, these are the rules that define the collective sense of a modern-day "egalitarian" in the context of a network of organizations and multiple social identities. The three commitments are:

- Working within the Democratic Party if and when the organization chooses to engage in partisan politics. This rule makes participation in electoral politics conditional, not mandatory, and it also leaves open if and how the organization may wish to participate in nonpartisan electoral politics at the local and county levels.
- Use planning through the market if the organization chooses to develop any economic programs. This rule leaves an emphasis on economic issues entirely up to individual organizations. At the same time, it states that organizations that advocate abolishing markets and relying on central planning would not be eligible for participation in the network.

• Strategic nonviolence is the only acceptable form of social movement activity. This rule is meant to exclude those who advocate violent tactics and strategies.

At the organizational level, the network can be coordinated to some extent by the many people who would be in two or more groups, which has worked well for many different types of endeavors in the United States. Members of two or more organizations carry new ideas from organization to organization, tell organizations about potential new leaders they have worked with in other organizations, and much else. As now, the network would have some degree of coordination through articles on movement activities in progressive and left-wing publications. It also could be integrated through informal meetings of leaders, but it is probably best to avoid any formal organization consisting only of leaders. Such an organization of organizations can contribute to the development of hierarchy.

Within this shared context, the network is most specifically coordinated when any given organization goes to other organizations in the network to ask them to join a specific project. Other organizations need join only if they think the project is worthwhile. In this way, only projects that are widely accepted receive large-scale support. Such a process takes time and requires compromises, but it helps to keep the Iron Law of Oligarchy at bay.

The egalitarian Democratic clubs (EDCs) would be one part of this network. They would have the same kind of constitutions and follow the three commitments. They would have to convince other organizations in the network to join them in any given campaign within the Democratic Party. In essence, then, the network as a whole would decide when and where to move into electoral politics through the EDCs, which of course would have many members in common with the other organizations. The network would also generate its own candidates, not simply endorse the person who appears to be the best liberal or the most charismatic progressive in the race. Otherwise, the goal of creating a set of politicians who are responsible to the movement would be lost. So would the point of using campaigns as a way to build a clear picture of who is us and who is them. It may also be the case that members of the movement would only think of themselves as "egalitarians" when they are acting together in the political arena, which means that their other social identities would be salient most of the time.

So, too, can individual trade unions join the network if they so desire. This book has spoken of a "liberal-labor alliance," but it has not put great stress on unions because they must be seen as just one part of an overall picture, not the starting point or the key organization. Many egalitarians would like to see unions take a more assertive political role in creating a more promising future for everyone who works for a salary or a wage, and they think that a primary focus on greater union organizing should be a major objective. However, unions more often than not function as "interest groups" that look out for their own members on issues concerning wages, hours, and working conditions. Moreover, and contrary to those who think renewed militancy is enough, it is very difficult to win organizing battles against corporations without major support from the government, as detailed historical case studies painfully reveal. Even when unions are already established, they cannot have a strong impact without a continuing alliance with a prounion-elected majority in the federal government.

Unions do play an important role in financing the Democratic Party and could be very helpful to egalitarian Democrats if they donated money for primary challenges, but they have an overriding interest in maintaining access to elected Democrats and to keeping some lines open to the Republicans. The American Federation of Labor and Congress of Industrial Organizations (AFL-CIO), as the umbrella group for most unions, may lend support for specific projects and provide a symbolic presence or thousands of marchers for some demonstrations, but its generally liberal leadership is often constrained by the need to compromise with its most conventional and conservative member unions. This is especially the case for several of the building trades unions, which can be very conservative on some issues. Furthermore, unions represent only 14 percent of all workers, and just under 10 percent of privately employed workers. Thus, many specific unions may be an important part of the network on some issues, but few of them are likely to play an active part in creating an egalitarian movement. It may be necessary to have union support eventually to go very far, but it would not be wise to wait until they are ready to start the ball rolling.

Once there are organizations working together that share the three commitments, the general movement then can grow through the addition of new members to existing organizations or adding new organizations. New organizations are accepted if and only if they have the three commitments built into their rules.

Are there examples of such a structure? In fact, this abstract outline is more or less a summary of how the living-wage and antisweatshop campaigns have been carried out. They are movements based on a variety of independent organizations that have decided to work together. The living-wage initiative, which calls on city and county governments to do business only with companies that pay what is necessary for a minimum standard of living in the area, is the product of the Association of Community Organizations for Reform Now (ACORN), a neighborhood organizing group, and the Service Employees International Union (SEIU), a service-industry union. ACORN and the SEIU have drawn churches, civil rights groups, women's organizations, and some unions into many dozens of local coalitions, which led to seventy-nine victories between 1994 and early 2002. Living-wage campaigns are usually aimed at the city council or county board of supervisors, but in New Orleans the coalition launched a citywide referendum to raise the minimum wage for everyone in the area to $6.15, $1 above the national minimum at the time. It won with an overwhelming 63 percent of the vote in early 2002, but the state's supreme court ruled six to one that cities cannot impose a wage for all local workers that is higher than the minimum wage set by the U.S. Congress.

Antisweatshop campaigns are first of all the creation of university campus-based organizations that demand that the university jackets, sweatshirts, and other apparel sold in campus stores be made by companies that pay living wages. They were started by student organizers who were trained by the AFL-CIO through its student-oriented institute called Union Summer, and they often draw in local unions and other grassroots organizations. Some antisweatshop groups also have branched out to fight for living wages for the service personnel on their campuses, which often means further union involvement. Using research, media presentations, picketing, sit-ins, boycotts, and hunger strikes, they have been successful on dozens of campus across the country since they began in 1997.

The organizations in these two separate, but overlapping, movements do not have the three commitments built into their rules, but those rules are implicit in what they do. First, they have not tried to start third parties, usually preferring to work in nonpartisan politics at the local level if they enter into electoral politics at all. Second, the very fact that the living-wage campaigns demand a "living wage" for those working for companies doing business with the government is an example of planning through the market. Third, these campaigns are nonviolent. Thus, it would not be hard for any of the organizations in the living-wage and antisweatshop campaigns to build the three commitments into their rules.

The feminist movement also has a highly decentralized and networked structure that starts with small support groups, turns to local-level projects, and comes together in nationwide organizations like the

National Organization for Women (NOW). The local groups do not control NOW, and NOW does not control the local groups, although it has local chapters. In effect, the organizations in the feminist network adhere to the three commitments, which is one reason for their successes. They have been loathe to advocate third parties, and their victories within the Democratic Party have created tensions within the Republican Party on abortion and affirmative action, and forced the Republicans to support more women candidates, albeit conservative women. Then, too, the movement believes in government planning through the market, as shown by its support of affirmative action and antidiscrimination laws. Most of its members also believe that the government has to support child care, social security, and their right to choose if they are going to be able to advance in their careers without taking time out to stay at home with young children, care for aging parents, or complete an unexpected pregnancy.

The global justice movement also has a decentralized type of structure, reflecting the antiauthoritarian thrust of the movement. However, the rejection of any formal rules by most organizations involved in street demonstrations, and their emphasis on direct democracy, makes them vulnerable to control through a combination of charisma and persistence. If the experiences of the late 1960s are any indication, they may come to suffer from a tyranny of structurelessness, which leads to invisible hierarchies and informal power structures that are somewhat masked by the claim that there are no leaders. In addition, the global justice movement has been divided over the issue of including property destruction as a part of direct action.

So, the basic structures are already there in the living-wage, antisweatshop, and feminist movements for a nonhierarchical egalitarian movement. They are also potentially present in the global justice movement if it can accept the need for leadership accountability and an exclusive focus on nonviolent direct action. The success of the first three movements is demonstrated by the fact that they do not feature any big names who hog the limelight. The main reason they have not created a nationwide network, I believe, is that most people do not want to be caught up in the highly divisive issues that are addressed by the three commitments. They do not want to hassle with Green Party enthusiasts or find themselves shunned by liberal Democrats, so they often avoid anything that smacks of partisan politics, with the exception of feminist groups. They do not want to enter into lengthy arguments about socialism with those who define themselves as socialists or revolutionary Marxists, so they usually avoid large umbrella coalitions where revolutionary Marxist front groups might gain a big role. They do not want to find themselves part of demonstrations or projects that involve people or groups who may decide to destroy property or provoke the police, so they stay home.

In short, people don't want to end up trapped by bullies, egotists, and power trippers, and they understand the Iron Law of Oligarchy. They want inverted power structures like the ones found in hunting and gathering societies. The organizational framework suggested in this chapter is therefore meant to create inverted power structures for modern times. If such structures proved safe and durable, many more people might feel comfortable in joining an egalitarian movement.

7

A NEW FOREIGN POLICY AND A NEW STANCE ON RELIGION

Egalitarians need to make adjustments in two further areas that loom large in American politics: foreign policy and organized religion. New perspectives on these emotionally charged issues would give egalitarians renewed legitimacy and openings to reach out to even more people.

The area of foreign policy is an especially difficult one for egalitarians, where there is nothing to gain and everything to lose as far as relating to the majority of citizens. Most Americans don't care much about other countries, and therefore don't know much about them, but they won't pay any attention to egalitarians unless they have a credible stance on the whole range of foreign policy issues. It is a crucial litmus test for many reasons, including fear of foreign nations, sentimental feelings about ancestral homelands, and, most of all, nationalistic pride. All of these concerns are multiplied by the frightening terrorist attacks on September 11, 2001.

What makes all this perilous for egalitarians is that they usually are internationalists, which leads them to be more interested in foreign issues, more respectful of other countries' viewpoints, and more willing to help other countries than the typical American. Even more, they are opposed to the domination of one nation-state by another, a form of hierarchy (imperialism) that existed long before either capitalism or the United States appeared on the scene. Internationalism and anti-imperialism do not mean that egalitarians are "anti-American," but they often face this accusation because they are not willing to go along with and applaud imperialist adventures. In the face of such criticisms, egalitarians can find themselves becoming increasingly antinationalist, which then can lead to a tendency to become even more critical of American foreign policy than otherwise might be the case. The result of these interactions and a hardening of positions can be isolation from everyday Americans.

But there is also something more going on that complicates, and in many ways distorts, an internationalist, anti-imperialist stance. It concerns the willingness to support and defend undemocratic regimes created in the name of communism. It is the defense of the Soviet Union, China, and other communist countries that most puzzled and angered liberals and moderates in the past, and in the process provided the right wing with one of its main clubs for beating on egalitarians as hypocrites who allegedly do not really care about freedom and democracy. Moreover, this defense of undemocratic regimes also generated enormous conflict among egalitarians themselves, leading to long-standing disagreements that made outreach to the rest of the citizenry even more difficult.

Worst of all, the past defense of communist countries has left present-day egalitarians with a one-dimension stance toward foreign policy issues: There should be no American interventions of any kind. The laudable principle of self-determination is made inviolate under all circumstances on all issues. Although plausible and sensible in the abstract, this general noninterventionism creates dilemmas when faced with horrors such as ethnic cleansing, mistreatment of women, unending ethnic–religious conflicts, and terrorism. Should the United States intervene against ethnic cleansing in the Balkan countries? Should it work for gender equality in post-Taliban Afghanistan, Saudi Arabia, and other highly sexist countries? Should it help to achieve a Palestinian state and at least some degree of autonomy for the Chechens, who have been fighting Russian invaders on and off since 1818? Should it actively search everywhere to capture terrorists who may use nuclear, chemical, or biological weapons to kill even more American and European civilians than were killed on September 11?

In order to answer these questions in a way that is consistent with egalitarian values, and to develop a new orientation on foreign policy in general, it is necessary to explain briefly how a rigidly noninterventionist policy developed on the left in the aftermath of the Bolshevik Revolution, and in the process divided and ultimately destroyed what is now known as the "Old Left." It's just history, I realize, but it is a tortured history that new egalitarians need to know in order to understand how some of the theorists they read and admire developed their ideas. Only after this tale is told is it possible to appreciate why a whole new approach to foreign policy is now needed.

Although the story begins with the internationalism and anti-imperialism embraced by most egalitarians, it soon becomes intertwined with key precepts of Marxism, whose strong internationalist ideals are one of its appeals to egalitarians. "Workers of the world, unite, you have nothing to lose but your chains," may be the most quoted phrase in the *Communist Manifesto*. Acting on this stirring call, Marxists have organized themselves into "internationals" from the outset, meaning organizations with committees or branches in several countries. The socialist parties in Europe founded an international in the 1880s, which the Socialist Party in America joined after it was formed in 1901. After the Bolshevik Revolution, Vladimir Lenin founded a new international to embrace parties that wanted to follow his insurrectionary strategy in other countries; three small new communist parties from the United States soon applied for membership. When Joseph Stalin ousted Leon Trotsky as a Bolshevik leader in the late 1920s, Trotsky founded another international, which persists to this day and plays a role in most antiwar demonstrations in Europe and the United States. Thus, it is not surprising that American egalitarians would be concerned about revolutions in the name of communism in Russia and China no matter how undemocratic their political regimes may have started out.

However, it was not simply internationalism that drew American leftists into the defense of foreign revolutions that did not immediately institute democratic regimes. This support also makes sense because of the Marxian idea that changes in the economic base of the social system are the main cause of changes in government and culture. Even when it is agreed by some Marxists that the government and culture can in turn influence the economic base, the economic system is still said to be determinative in the final analysis. According to this theory, then, an economy planned for the benefit of everyone should naturally lead to democracy; a socialist economy leads to a democratic polity. Marxists therefore had the theoretical hope that these underdeveloped communist countries would eventually become more democratic. In the meantime, undemocratic communist governments were excused as the unfortunate and temporary by-product of economic underdevelopment and hostile attacks by capitalist countries. This hope turned out to have no chance of realization, as explained in chapter 3, because of the difficulties of managing a centrally planned economy and the tendencies to authoritarianism within a planning bureaucracy, which actually reinforced the worst tendencies in the Soviet Union and China.

But it wasn't just a matter of internationally oriented egalitarians believing that a centrally planned socialist economic system would shape the political system in a democratic direction. Many pro-Soviet and pro-China Marxists also had a strong dislike of capitalism, believing that it was the most immoral and crassest of economic systems, even though they praised its productive capabilities for laying the foundations for socialism. In their view, it was time for the system to be replaced because it completely exploited and dehumanized workers. That pressing moral necessity based on sympathy for the working class came to justify a policy of any means necessary to get rid of capitalism in a context where democracy presumably would follow relatively soon thereafter. Moreover, the desire to replace capitalism in any way possible was heightened by Lenin's new analysis of modern-day imperialism as an even more pernicious stage of capitalism. According to this analysis, the capitalists in Europe and the United States were responsible for the underdevelopment of the Third World, including Russia. The Third World was being ripped off by the advanced capitalist world without receiving anything much in return.

Based on these predispositions, the clinching argument comes from glowing eyewitness testimony concerning the early successes of the various revolutions. As shown in a study of all the first-person accounts provided by Americans about their visits to new communist countries, this pattern repeated itself almost exactly throughout the twentieth century despite devastating revelations about the earlier revolutions. The basic story runs as follows. Prominent American egalitarians are invited to see for themselves shortly after the revolution. They are met by charming and sophisticated people who often speak good English and are knowledgeable about American culture. They are taken to model factories and farms, and have meetings with political leaders, who flatter them greatly. Based on this limited experience in a country where they don't know the language, they are convinced of a positive future for the revolution. They return home to give enthusiastic speeches and write glowing accounts. Since they have been there and have seen for themselves, they are trusted by fellow egalitarians at home. Support for the revolution is now solidified.

Based on this complex mix of values, theory, and eyewitness testimony, many of the most committed Marxists in the United States became members of the Communist Party (CP), which identified itself closely with the Soviet Union and always followed its lead when it came to key foreign policy issues. Although most CP members concentrated their efforts in the 1930s and 1940s on organizing at the local level for unionization, racial integration, and basic civil rights, the party's constantly changing stance on foreign policy often undercut their efforts and created tensions with other left activists. For example, due to instructions from the Soviet Union, the party attempted to form new unions independent of the American Federation of Labor between 1929 and 1935, and also vigorously criticized New Deal president Franklin D. Roosevelt. These efforts alienated the established trade unions and those egalitarians who supported Roosevelt.

Then, in 1935, in response to the Nazi takeover in Germany, Moscow told communist parties everywhere to join antifascist coalitions, which allowed the American CP to do what it was inclined to do anyhow: to support both Roosevelt and mainstream unionism. This change in line made it possible for the party to supply many of the organizers who built the Congress of Industrial Organizations (CIO) after 1936. The CP soon controlled twelve to fifteen of the forty unions in the CIO, making up about 20 percent of the overall membership, and had influence in some of the larger unions as well. It was a hopeful moment for a left-liberal-labor coalition within the Democratic Party that seemed to be making progress. Leftists and strong liberals worked together to elect socialists and liberals to office as Democrats in much the way advocated earlier in this book.

But the needs of the Soviet Union intervened once again. The CP alienated liberals, socialists, and most of organized labor in 1939 when it supported the Nazi–Soviet Pact, suddenly turning against Roosevelt as an alleged war monger and arguing against rearmament. Twenty-two months later, when the Nazis invaded the Soviet Union, American communists became such strong supporters of all-out war production that they would not support strikes or even the March on Washington planned by the African American socialist A. Philip Randolph to demand fair play for blacks. By that point, the party had lost all respect from any political groups that were left of center, but it still had a stronghold in the CIO.

Deference to the Soviet Union on foreign policy put a complete end to any remnants of the left-liberal-labor coalition in 1948 when Moscow, reacting to the Marshall Plan, unexpectedly told the American CP to support the attempt to build a third party by Henry Wallace, who had served as vice president from 1941 to 1945 after seven years as secretary of agriculture. Wallace's effort was supported because he opposed the looming Cold War and thought peaceful coexistence was possible. This involvement in the Progressive Party led to the expulsion of communist leaders from the CIO for breaking with the CIO's policy of supporting the Democrats. CIO leaders who were communists either had to renounce the CP or be kicked out of the CIO. Neither the CP or the Old Left in general ever recovered from the divisions and defeats set in motion by the Wallace campaign.

However, as suggested earlier in this chapter, this convoluted history did leave a foreign policy legacy. Although relatively small in number, the pro-Soviet theorists in and around the party had a very large impact on American egalitarian thinking on foreign policy that persists to this day. They had this impact primarily through an elaboration of the Marxist theory of economic imperialism, in which they blamed the United States for the spread of capitalism and for opposing socialism. Whatever the truth of this claim, in fact the theory was most of all meant as a defense of the Soviet Union and its attempt to extend its version of socialism to other countries. It opposed American interventionism out of the justified fear that the United States would challenge the Soviet Union and its allies, but it did not oppose Soviet support for leftists in other countries because of the assumed superiority of socialism over capitalism. What the Soviet Union did was said to be emancipatory, but what the United States did was reactionary meddling. In short, Marxist and Marxist-influenced American leftists did not have a consistent anti-imperialist stance. They opposed capitalist economic imperialism, but not Soviet political imperialism. They, therefore, looked like apologists for undemocratic regimes to many Americans.

This legacy helped shape the New Left's response to the Vietnam War and eventually split the antiwar movement into radical and liberal factions, each with its own separate strategies and demonstrations. Instead of opposing the war as unnecessary or unwinnable, both of which turned out to be accurate assessments, as serious analysts at the time already knew, Students for a Democratic Society and it allies came to identify with the guerillas and their National Liberation Front. As one leading participant in these events later put it, "Much of the leadership, and some of the rank and file—it is hard to say exactly how many—slid into romance with the other side." As early as December 1965, two radical antiwar leaders visited Hanoi and came away greatly impressed in the usual manner of previous American observers of foreign revolutions. Within a year or two, however, one of these visitors realized he had been "snookered" by the North Vietnamese when they told him there were no North Vietnamese troops in South Vietnam. He then decided to concentrate on domestic social issues, but most of his fellow radicals soon turned to violent disruption. They did so with the hope that they could hamper the war effort. They chose this course even though they knew such tactics would alienate the overwhelming majority of Americans. They were now acting on behalf of Vietnamese guerrillas, which was a long way from the effort by the peace movement in general to convince the American majority to oppose the war.

Due to this long history of supporting all anticapitalist insurgents across the globe, most egalitarians now oppose virtually all American foreign policy initiatives in the name of anti-imperialism. This historic tendency is reinforced by the many revolutionary Marxists active within the present-day global justice and antiwar coalitions. Egalitarians therefore call for a noninterventionist foreign policy. They point out that people should have the right of self-determination. It is a one-dimensional stance that does not reflect the complexity of the world situation, the mixed effects of American foreign policy, or the potential positive impacts of relatively slight changes in American foreign policy. Due to its overemphasis on capitalism and imperialism, and its tendency to minimize the role of nation-states as power actors, it also misunderstands the nature of most ethnic and religious conflicts around the world, especially since the end of the Cold War. It is not possible to reduce the multifaceted process of globalization to conflicts over land ownership, labor rights, and capital flows.

An egalitarian foreign policy should be based on an attempt to realize egalitarian values to the greatest extent possible, independent of what the American government is proposing. For the foreseeable future, this means human rights for everyone in every nation-state, the right to have and participate in a nation-state, and the greatest possible equality that can be achieved within a reconstructed market system based on planning through the market. Once egalitarians have staked out this position based on their own values and analysis, they then can support, modify, or reject American foreign policy initiatives, rather than simply opposing all of them as imperialistic.

The area of human rights is the best starting point to make the case for a differentiated stance toward American foreign policy. Egalitarians believe that everyone should have the right to belong to the religion of their choice, to organize political parties, and to join trade unions. They believe there should be equality for women, racial and ethnic minorities, and gays and lesbians. Although many of these values are also embodied in European and American ideals, that does not make it ethnocentric for Americans to advocate them. Nor does it imply that Europeans and Americans are somehow naturally more enlightened. After all, it took many hundreds of years of wars, religious persecution, ethnic conflicts, and more recently race riots and civil rights movements for some degree of religious tolerance and democratic participation to emerge in Europe and the United States.

Whatever the historical reasons for the ideals about human rights, freedom, and democratic participation projected by the United States, the fact is that this aspect of American culture is embraced by many people across the world as a beacon of hope. In addition, the government has proclaimed in recent years that it engages other countries partially in terms of how they do on human rights issues. In theory, a country has to meet human rights standards in order to receive American foreign aid. Needless to add, the government does not always act on the basis of these professed ideals.

Since the values of egalitarians and the American government coincide on human rights issues, American egalitarians should express their support for the emphasis on human rights in American foreign policy. There can be calls for gender equality and religious tolerance in all countries without any apologies about allegedly imposing mere American values, and there can be criticism of any country that practices sexism, racism, homophobia, or religious persecution. There need be no hesitation about advocating the use of strategic nonviolence in currently violent conflicts where the government is at least quasi democratic.

Egalitarians should also create pressure to make sure that the American government lives up to its professed ideals more often. They should support Amnesty International, Human Rights Watch, and other human rights organizations that many of them tended to ignore in the past. They should back United Nations (UN) initiatives on human rights and insist that all its member nations, including the United States, come quickly into compliance with the rules they have agreed to, but often ignore. There should be no more apologies for the Third World countries that violate basic human rights, including communist or formerly communist countries.

It is perhaps especially important for egalitarians to advocate the right to democratic participation within all countries and insist that the American government support transitions to democracy. Such a policy would bring egalitarians into frequent conflict with foreign policy makers if past experience is any indication. Indeed, as recently as April 2002 the Bush administration tacitly accepted the overthrow of the elected president of Venezuela by wealthy conservative elites because he is a populist who is often critical of the United States. When the low-income people of Venezuela and the leaders of other Latin American countries forced the deposed president's return to power, Condoleezza Rice, Bush's national security advisor, setting a new record for arrogance and gall by a super power, warned the restored president to "respect constitutional processes."

Egalitarians should be especially sensitive to insisting on respect for the rights of those in the political minority in newly developing democracies. Too many seemingly democratic elections have led to the crushing of the losers in the past fifty years, who are often ethnic or racial minorities within their respective countries. It is therefore completely certain that the democratic conditions for an election have to be met before any elections are held. For egalitarians, that should mean mandatory monitoring of elections by teams from democratic countries or from the UN. To set the right example and provide an international context for all elections, such teams should be sent to the United States, Canada, and European democracies as well as newly developing democracies. It may even mean sending foreign or UN troops to new democracies to avoid bloody election aftermaths. There have to be "managed political openings," as one expert on democracy puts it.

Within this context, the American government should be pushed to use sanctions in support of democracy within repressive countries that are its close allies, just as egalitarians did in the successful fight against apartheid in South Africa. Here, the best current case in point would be the undemocratic oil-producing Middle Eastern countries, which are propped up and defended by the American military against their own people and rival authoritarian states. In the aftermath of September 11, such pressures also can be seen as acting in the national interest because these repressive states breed terrorists who are sometimes financed surreptitiously by billionaire oil sheiks. Egalitarians cannot allow the United States to continue uncritical support of these regimes. Nor can they allow these regimes to continue to play a double game—friends of the United States and major supporters of its enemies.

Moving beyond the issues of human rights and democratic rights within emerging nation-states, egalitarians should insist that oppressed peoples have a right to a nation-state. The most murderous and enduring disputes in the world today involve the thoroughly modern desire to have a nation-state on the part of the Palestinians, Chechens, and many other oppressed ethnic groups. One power analyst estimates that as many as one-third of the major disputes in the world today involve this issue. These insurgencies are often portrayed as religious ones, but they usually are rooted in secular nationalism and use religion as one of their key motivators and justifications. To take the obvious example, Palestinian suicide bombers may or may not talk about their religious beliefs, but they are seeking self-determination in the form of a Palestinian state. Such demands cannot be understood in terms of the spread of capitalism or attributed to economic imperialism.

In an ideal world, the UN would have the will and strength to help mediate these disputes and find peaceful compromises. However, it is clear that this is not going to happen, partly because the United States is not willing to risk losing any control to an international body, but also because undemocratic regimes have at the least a veto power at the UN. To the degree that the United States enters into these disputes, it is going to do so through coalitions it organizes. It was Bill Clinton in 1993, not George W. Bush in 2001, who told the UN that the United States would act "multilaterally when possible but unilaterally when necessary." What, then, should egalitarians advocate in the face of unpleasant alternatives? They should first of all continue to urge that the United States support the UN in settling these disputes, but they should also advocate American intervention if they cannot pressure the government to work through the UN. Then they should work to have the United States side with the aggrieved party, not with the repressive power.

Once again, the Israeli–Palestinian conflict is a prototypical case. Following the Holocaust and World War II, European Jews intensified their campaign for a Jewish state, and the British and Americans backed them in this effort, an example of how the American government should react to the quest for self-determination. It is also understandable that the Palestinians would want a state of their own for the same reasons, and they will never give up until they have one. It has been clear to everyone for a long time, including most Israelis and Palestinians, that the advanced capitalist countries, led by the United States, are going to have to force the two peoples to accept a negotiated settlement in which the Israelis pull back to their 1967 boundaries (as modified only by minor mutually agreeable territorial swaps). In exchange, the Palestinians—and other Arabs—must recognize the right of Israel to exist. Israel would have to evacuate all settlements in occupied territories and the Palestinians would have to accept negotiated limitations on the right of refugees to return to land inside Israel's boundaries in exchange for financial compensation.

The necessary American role in bringing about this solution is advocated by egalitarians and liberals within the American Jewish community. It is the role advocated by former president Jimmy Carter. It was the role that President Clinton seemed to be close to fulfilling when time ran out on his presidency. It is the role that President Bush originally walked away from because he and his party shun an interventionist role and because the negotiations were too closely connected to Clinton. In effect, the Republicans abandoned the kind of role that egalitarians should be advocating. Republicans deserve much criticism for their short-sighted nationalistic politics, which allowed a deadly ethnic–religious conflict over statehood to erupt into bloodshed once again.

Beyond conflicts over human rights and the right to have a state, there are many economic battles involving land, labor, and capital that come with the spread of American, European, and Japanese capitalism to the rest of the world. It is here that the Marxian anti-imperialist critique fits into the picture. The American government, in its role as leader of the capitalist world, too often sides with local landlords and capitalists against indigenous peoples, landless peasants, and workers. It almost always supports regimes that repress their own citizens. It advocates a set of economic policies— maximum reliance on the market, low tariffs, minimal welfare benefits, and austere government budgets to avoid inflation—that are ruinous to developing countries. Along with its allies, the United States stands behind and finances the international agencies that carry out the policies favored by multinational corporations.

Egalitarians have to oppose the American government on virtually all of its foreign economic policies, but not simply as anticapitalists, anti-imperialists, or opponents of the World Trade Organization (WTO). They have to challenge these policies through the advocacy of a reconstructed market system that can make use of relatively free trade among countries with developed economies, while providing aid, subsidies, and protections for the economies in developing countries. Most importantly, they have to work to elect a congressional majority of egalitarian Democrats and at least a moderate Democrat to the White House. Under these circumstances, foreign economic policies would reflect the possibility of a more egalitarian market system. Otherwise, American foreign economic policy will continue to be an expression of the low-tax, antigovernment policy regime that is also the Republican vision for the United States. The biggest favor that egalitarians could do for the rest of the world is to be successful in domestic electoral politics.

In the context of challenging these austere foreign economic policies in the name of a more egalitarian market system, many of the specific proposals already developed by egalitarians and reformers would come into play. Less developed countries should be encouraged to permit unions, set minimum wages, provide welfare benefits, control capital flows in and out of the country, and institute progressive taxation. There should be controls of various kinds on multinational corporations, and American-based multinationals should not receive tax breaks from the United States for taxes they pay in other countries, as they currently do. There should be much higher levels of American, European, and Japanese foreign economic aid to less developed countries, and perhaps especially to those countries that the United States undermined during the Cold War with aid to repressive armies (e.g., Guatemala) or help for terrorists (e.g., the contras in Nicaragua). The commitment of 0.7 percent of the gross domestic product to such aid, as proposed by the UN, should be advocated, a sevenfold increase from the meager 0.1 percent currently contributed by the United States. More of this aid should be funneled through the UN. There are also difficult issues, on which there is no consensus among leftists, as to whether the International Monetary Fund, World Bank, and WTO should be significantly changed or simply abolished.

However, it is beyond my knowledge and purpose to enter into debates about specific policies relating to the many regions, countries, and economies in the world, or about exactly what to do about international economic institutions. My point here is that there is a solid basis for a foreign policy based in egalitarian values that stresses democracy as well as internationalist values. It includes a critique of imperialism, but does not stop there.

This egalitarian orientation to foreign policy turns out to be interventionist as well as anti-imperialist, not simply anti-interventionist. It is interventionist on human rights because they are universal values, not simply Western ones. It is interventionist for the right of self-determination through nation-states because that is the only way such conflicts will ever be resolved peacefully. It is interventionist for a reconstructed market system because the current American economic policies are undesirable and the socialist plans embraced by many leaders in the global justice movement will not work.

The collapse of the Soviet Union makes it possible for egalitarians to rethink their foreign policy legacy. Now there is little or nothing out there for them to defend. Moreover, such rethinking becomes imperative due to the events of September 11 and the increasingly obvious role of the United States as the main guarantor of stability in an era of potentially devastating terrorism.

A STANCE ON RELIGION

In comparison to foreign policy, the issues facing egalitarians concerning religion are more straightforward and easier to handle. They have also become less contentious and problematic over the past decade. Here, the problem is that some present-day egalitarians, who are disproportionately secularists, have a strong tendency to engage in needless conflict with organized religion. They do so not only because many of them see religion itself as irrational, but because they think Christian churches, Catholic and Protestant alike, are on the side of the status quo. They tend to think this in spite of the involvement of faith-based groups in many egalitarian and humanitarian projects, including projects that challenge corporate power and/or support low-wage workers.

Religion is the way in which many human beings search for two separate but overlapping goals: meaning and community. It is as old as the species and is likely to be around in one form or another until the species vanishes. It offers answers to puzzling and painful questions relating to death, guilt, and the reasons for conscious self-awareness. In its modern forms, it also tries to reproduce the cooperation, intimacy, and common bonds that were the basis of the small hunting and gathering groups in which human beings lived for tens of thousands of years. Religious communities create an automatic in-group that is separate from the workplace and political arena. They are not going to go away if class societies are replaced by classless ones.

While it is true that in recent times most religions have been on the side of the powerful, and that fundamentalist Protestant churches are currently a key part of the Republican right, this is not always the case, which makes any attack on religion even more counterproductive. Indeed, some of the major egalitarian activists of the nineteenth century came from organized religion. In the twentieth century, Quakers, Jews, and members of African American churches in the South were among the leading egalitarians in the feminist, union, and civil rights movements. In addition, many of the recent anticorporate activists and supporters of Central American refugees are from liberal Protestant denominations and parts of the Catholic Church.

For the most part, we think of those in organized religion as believers who are searching for meaning, but in fact many are there for the comfort and support that is needed in the face of death and for the sense of intimate community that is needed for highly emotional and meaningful occasions like initiations into adulthood or marriage. This distinction between meaning and community within organized religion is expressed perfectly by one of the great physicists of modern times, Freeman Dyson, who describes himself as a "practicing Christian," not a believing one. He completely rejects all theologies and finds science a very satisfactory meaning context, but he nonetheless belongs to a Christian church as a way to participate in a purposeful community.

Given the diversity of meanings and practices that people bring to their religions, it does not make sense to respond to them as if they were all doing the same thing. All that egalitarians need to insist on from organized religious groups is tolerance for the right to choose a religion, and for the right to be nonreligious if one so chooses. This readily follows from American pluralistic values, but it is a tall order historically, as decades and centuries of religious wars in Europe, the Near East, and India reveal. It also remains a very contentious matter in the United States, as seen when the issue is tolerance for non-Christian religions or atheists. Still, the overall acceptance of the pluralistic view is revealed in increasing intermarriage among all types of Christians, and between Jews and Christians. These and other bonds have created bridges among the religious groups.

This live-and-let-live stance toward organized religion does not mean acceptance of all the practices of a religious group. On the contrary, it creates a more powerful basis from which to challenge the negative aspects of specific religions that infringe on the rights of others. On right to choose issues, for example, it remains proper and necessary to oppose the efforts of the Catholic hierarchy and fundamentalist Protestants, both of which have been outrageous in their support of restrictions on abortion rights in the face of American pluralist values and an endorsement of this right by a majority of Protestants and Catholics. It is also necessary for egalitarians to oppose the gender discrimination that is practiced in most religions and to criticize Christian opposition to sex education and contraception. In short, it is not the search for meaning and community that should be under attack, but specific practices that often contradict the values of the religious group and also contradict American pluralist values. By making this distinction, egalitarian activists can be even more critical and effective in their challenges to antiegalitarian religious practices.

The issues addressed in this chapter are the final pieces in a new egalitarian program. This new program gives egalitarians the potential to reach a majority of Americans without any apologies, distractions, hesitations, or fears of immediate rejection. There is now only one more problem to consider: the wasted time and energy that goes into complaining about the media.

8

STOP BLAMING THE MEDIA

Like everyone else, egalitarians have a strong tendency to blame the media for their failures. Media power becomes an excuse for not considering the possibility that much of the egalitarian analysis is unappealing to most people—third parties, centrally planned economies, violent tactics, a tendency to rely on charismatic leaders, uncritical admiration of foreign revolutions, and disdain for organized religion. None of these has any appeal to average Americans, and it is not the media that created this negative reaction.

Today, the main culprit is said to be television, with its misleading or distracting images, but the complaint goes back to the days when there were only newspapers. It leads to endless dissection of every media story to find any mistakes and distortions. Blaming the media reinforces any tendency toward conspiratorial thinking. It crowds out creative thinking about how to make use of the media as part of strategic nonviolent campaigns.

To take a recent instance, Ralph Nader's book on his 2000 presidential campaign blames the media for most of his failures. He tells of the many times that inept reporters asked if he was worried about throwing the election to George W. Bush and the Republicans. He thinks that's an irrelevant question—only the issues and programs matter. The person with the best platform should win, with no thought of the underlying electoral coalitions that support the Democratic and Republican Parties. But the reporters' question actually reflected the central power issue in the campaign, the potential for the Green Party to ensure victory for the Republicans.

Nader even blames the media for violence by demonstrators in recent years. Newspapers and television don't give fair coverage, and therefore impulsive people resort to violence to gain some attention. At the same time, Nader is devastating in his assessment of the demonstrations where violence does erupt. He says that "the power structures know these 'we protest and demand' rallies are harmless vetting of steam," and that the demonstrators' message is "lost" within the "mock wars" between protestors and police. If the message is "lost," then perhaps the violence is pointless in the first place. Nader should have said and done much more to reinforce the necessity of sustained strategic nonviolence.

Nader's book has a long chapter fulminating against the Commission on Presidential Debates because it excluded him from the presidential debates. He clearly believes that the media exposure from appearing in the debates would have improved his vote total considerably. Everything he says about the commission and its complicity with corporations and the media is true, as is his point that the candidates of the two major parties really call the shots. But it is a trivial revelation when it comes to what Nader claims is his major focus: building a strong anticorporate, egalitarian social movement in the United States with the help of the electoral system. It wasn't exclusion from the debates that kept his vote totals low, but the rules of the electoral system.

The general leftist view of the media begins with the fact that ownership and control of the media are highly concentrated, and growing more so all the time. It also stresses that the media are based on advertising dollars, which makes them sensitive to the concerns of big corporate advertisers. The media are also said to be biased because they rely on easy sources of information like government officials, corporate leaders, and experts. Constant criticism of the media by their advertisers and other corporate leaders keep them in line, as do shouts of "communism" and "anti-Americanism" when they print something the powers that be do not like. Finally, the media are said to play a big role in setting the agenda in terms of what issues people think are important enough for the government to address.

There is much to be said for this overall analysis, but it greatly overstates the case. It also ignores the many openings that are available to egalitarians when they learn how to use the media for their own purposes. In addition, it overlooks the way in which the media can be bypassed on some occasions.

Take the issue of media concentration. Concentration of ownership does not automatically mean that the range of opinions available through the media are narrowed. To assume this is to ignore the more basic question of how the news is produced by journalists and editors. For example, a study of large newspaper chains by a journalism professor suggests concentration may have less negative effects than leftists fear. Based on a content analysis of several editions, he first of all found that large newspapers and newspaper chains are more likely than small local newspapers to publish editorials and letters that deal with local issues or are critical of mainstream groups and institutions. Furthermore, he found that a wider range of opinions appears in the chain newspapers, including critical ones. Finally, using survey responses from 409 journalists at 223 newspapers, he found that their reporters and editors report high levels of autonomy.

The concern about media concentration does not address the small circulations suffered by the many left-wing magazines not owned by the major media. They often have had substantial funding from millionaire liberals and leftists, certainly enough to make themselves and their viewpoints known to millions of potential readers through mass mailings, but few people subscribe. At a moment when *Time* and *Newsweek* have circulations of 4.2 and 3.3 million, respectively, their closest equivalents on the left, *Mother Jones, The Nation,* and *The Progressive,* have circulations of 148,000, 97,000, and 36,000, respectively. The sad truth of the matter is that very few people are interested in what these magazines have to say, which means that the egalitarian programs offered so far are not very attractive or convincing for most people.

Although the big media are first and foremost concerned with making a profit, which of course gives them much commonality with other businesses, there are nonetheless differences on some issues between media executives and corporate leaders that can be exploited. For example, leaders in the mass media tend to be more moderate on foreign policy and domestic issues than corporate executives. On questions concerning the environment, which are very sensitive to corporate leaders, the media pros hold the same views as people from liberal organizations. To counter what they see as a liberal bias, corporations therefore run their own large advocacy statements in major newspapers.

Supporting the critique by leftists, there is experimental evidence from laboratory studies suggesting that television may have a role in setting the policy agenda. For example, when researchers place a story first on the evening news, or repeat it several times during the course of a week, people are more likely to think of those issues as more important. However, there is also real-world evidence that the news is often not watched even though the television is on and that people don't remember much of what they do see. The declining audiences for news programs lead to more and more emphasis on human interest stories, so the news is increasingly a form of entertainment. Several other studies suggest that most people actually retain more politically relevant information from what they read in newspapers and magazines. In addition, people seem to screen out information that does not fit with their preconceptions, and they rely on people they know in developing their opinions.

Studies of media content find it is not all to corporate liking. For example, there is a great emphasis on bad news and sensationalism, with a special emphasis on crime and disasters, which corporate leaders criticize because it paints a negative picture of American society. They may have a point: Studies demonstrate that people are influenced by negative news. The more crime news people watch, the more likely they are to overestimate the actual amount of crime, overestimate African American involvement in violent crime, favor more money for crime prevention, and favor the death penalty. These findings are also of interest because they suggest that the media's focus on any violence that occurs at protest demonstrations is not peculiar to the activities of leftists.

Sometimes the emphasis on violence can even be of benefit to egalitarian activists, as shown when the media picked up on the violence of the vigilantes, Ku Klux Klan, and police in opposing the civil rights movement. Some media analysts believe that the media became the movement's ally because people outside the South were outraged by what they saw. Nor could corporate leaders and government officials trying to compete with the Soviet Union in the Third World tolerate the rest of the world seeing these antidemocratic actions against people of color. Since trying to suppress freedom of the press was not an option, the rich and powerful had to condemn the violence in the South.

There is also evidence that people sometimes ignore overt attempts by the media to influence them. This is best seen in several well-known instances. For example, most newspapers were against the reelection of Franklin D. Roosevelt in 1936, but he won by a landslide. The media were against the reelection of Harry Truman in 1948, but he squeezed by in an upset victory. Led by the Washington pundits who appear on all the television opinion shows, the media were eager for the impeachment of Bill Clinton in 1998, with over 140 newspapers calling for his resignation, but a strong majority of the American public shocked the experts by opposing impeachment despite a highly negative opinion of his personal behavior. People decided on their own that there is a difference between job performance and personal morality. One polling expert even thinks that the media campaign against the president may have backfired by increasing public resentment toward the media.

Despite the general conservative biases of newspaper owners, there are studies showing that the journalists who actually produce the news are by and large independent professionals who make use of the freedom of the press that was won for them by courageous journalists of the past, often in battles with the federal government. This independence is first of all seen in the many stories on corporate and government wrongdoing developed in the long tradition of investigative journalism, which always has been strongly resisted by corporate and political leaders alike. Thanks to their great resources, the major newspapers do as many critical studies of corporate malfeasance and government favoritism to big business as activists or scholars. Their stories provide much of the grist for the left mill, as can be seen in the footnotes in any indictment of the American power structure.

Moreover, thanks to the willingness of journalists to report on the events of the day, the media are a key element in the success formula of the small bands of lawyers and experts who function as reformers on specific issues. These reformers develop information on the issue of concern to them, find a way to present that information at just the right moment in one or another governmental setting, such as congressional hearings, and then count on press releases, press conferences, and staged events to encourage the media to spread their story. In short, their formula for success is information plus good timing plus use of the media. There is ample evidence that this formula is an effective one, showing once again that a few focused activists can have an impact out of all proportion to their numbers or resources if they know how to use the media.

Thus, contrary to their complaints, egalitarians have a great many contacts and friends in the media. It even can be argued that one key to Nader's success down through the decades has been the media coverage his efforts have received, which has been overwhelmingly positive. Contrary to his annoyance, the fact that he was ignored when he ran for president on a third-party ticket is not a media plot. This neglect reflected the irrelevance to which he had condemned himself. However, when polls began to show that his few percent of the vote might matter in a few key states, the coverage naturally focused on his potential role as a spoiler for the Democrats because that was the most relevant point of his campaign in the eyes of most people. When Nader and his supporters complain about the nature of the media coverage, they are actually demanding that the media abandon an independent journalistic stance and champion their cause by reporting what they want reported. This is in effect what people from left, right, and center constantly do: attack the media with the hope that they will bend in their direction, and then blame the media if their program fails.

If egalitarians could bring the role of the media into a more balanced perspective, they could expend less energy attacking and analyzing them, and more effort figuring out how to make creative use of them as part of specific nonviolent campaigns. Since egalitarians seem to be most annoyed with the media for exaggerating leftist violence, maybe that is another reason to eliminate violent and destructive tactics from egalitarian social movements. Within a nonviolence context, the media might also be of more use in insurgent campaigns in Democratic primaries than egalitarians generally believe because of their attraction to uphill struggles by valiant underdogs.

As the leftist critiques emphasize, the media can magnify the message of the powerful and trivialize and marginalize the claims of the powerless. But the media don't cause some people to be powerful and some people to be powerless. They have many highly professional and insightful journalists who usually do a good job under the difficult circumstances of murky events, unwilling sources, and political pressures from right, left, and center. Blaming the media draws attention away from the failed policies of American egalitarians. The media are not part of the out-group. They are a third party to the struggle that can be used to good effect on many issues and should be cultivated. It is time to stop complaining about the media and adopt a new program with some life in it.

9

MAKING THE FUTURE YOURS

Modern-day egalitarians inherit a highly contradictory history that they continue to embody and repeat in their current activities. On the one hand, at any given moment the large-scale projects that most deeply interest them—new third parties, socialism, or a complete unionization of the work-force—usually end up as failures that are deeply disappointing for the activists. On the other hand, they are at the same time playing important roles as catalysts in movements that lead to enduring advances for women, blue-collar workers, people of color, and gays and lesbians. The dreary parts of this history are unknown to most egalitarians because leftist intellectuals would just as soon ignore them or explain them away, making it more likely that the mistakes will be repeated. And the good parts are too soon over-looked, taken for granted, or co-opted by the mainstream as something it has always favored.

Yes, hindsight is easy, but it can be useful in the context of general principles. The leftists of the 1930s might have become a real influence in the Democratic Party if so many of them hadn't followed the Communist Party line and supported the Nazi–Soviet Pact in 1939 and the Henry Wallace campaign of 1948. The young civil rights activists in the Student Nonviolent Coordinating Committee and the New Leftists in Students for a Democratic Society were just starting to have a real impact in the 1960s when they seemingly gave up on the American people and resorted to violent tactics, thereby alienating the great majority and setting themselves up for government repression. When the activists of the late 1990s suddenly started to have some success again, they lost most of their momentum because of those who engaged in property destruction or battles with the police at anti–World Trade Organization demonstrations. Then they finished themselves off for the time being by following Ralph Nader and the Greens in their hopeless attempt to build a new third party.

These blunders shout out the obvious lessons backed up by systematic studies in political science, sociology, and history: Stop with the third parties already, forget about centralized planning and doing away with the market system, no more violence, and don't blame the media for everything that goes wrong.

But what if no big improvements occur even though these suggestions are taken to heart? What then? That's one reason why this book praises and encourages single-issue campaigns around a livable wage, keeping toxic waste plants out of neighborhoods, or preserving specific habitats and places of beauty. They allow egalitarians to win battles on specific issues that make a difference in people's daily lives while biding their time as far as bigger changes are concerned. Just as earlier egalitarian activists helped usher in women's suffrage, industrial unions, civil rights legislation for African Americans and women, and greater protection of the environment, so too can today's new activists ensure the preservation of social security, improve government support for health care, fight for clean air, and much else while at the same time campaigning for large-scale changes. Being a catalyst and organizer for specific movements is an honorable and gratifying path. Indeed, as this book stresses, this is the best role possible for egalitarians who want to avoid the traps of elitism. Power is best challenged by those who do not seek power for themselves.

Still, honorable or not, one of the greatest difficulties facing the pathways laid out in this book is that they may not seem heroic or pure enough to the dedicated activists whose energy would be necessary to carry them through. Especially in the case of those who are young and just starting out, the hope may be for something that seems to require more confrontation and bravery. However, those with such urges can be assured that most Democrats would be deeply upset if they were challenged from precincts to president in party primaries. They would be restrained in their behavior to some extent by the desire to have egalitarian votes in the regular election, but their anger would be visible enough to astonish anyone looking for confrontation. It would also take extraordinary efforts to overcome the racial divide in the southern states and create the liberal black–white voting coalitions that are essential to any attempt at large-scale social change in the United States. Moreover, the program to reconstruct the market system, tame though it may sound to some potential activists, would be resisted mightily by moderate Democrats, Republicans, and the corporate-conservative coalition, and they would still scream all their scare words from "communist" to "secular humanist." Nor is the practice of strategic nonviolence a walk in the park. It takes far more courage, training, and discipline to participate in a sit-in, to strike, or to block access in the face of police and angry opponents than it does to throw rocks or plant bombs.

Although there would be great opposition to a new egalitarian movement, it is true that these pathways bypass the usual charges against egalitarians. After all, you are

- Not "spoilers" for the Democrats, but fellow Democrats, albeit of a different stripe
- Not against the market per se, and hence not socialists or communists
- Not advocates of violent tactics or armed struggle, and hence not pro-violence anarchists or revolutionaries
- Not opposed to religion as an institution for meaning and community, but simply fierce opponents of political intrusions carried out in the name of specific religions

Instead, that is, you are egalitarian Democrats who believe in planning through the market, strategic nonviolence, and religious freedom for all, including those who are nonreligious. The trick is to use this starting point to get under the power structure's ideological radar while at the same time knowing that your value system is intact and can provide the energy for sustained organizing and disrupting. From there, anyone who shares your basic egalitarian values and platform should be welcomed into your movement. The corporate-conservative coalition and the Republican Party are the clear opponents of this program, and they will do everything in their power to discredit it. They are the out-group. However, specific individuals should not be under suspicion whatever their social class, gender, color, sexual orientation, or previous political beliefs until they have proven themselves guilty by opposing egalitarian programs and candidates.

Would this program win if it were tried? Maybe not, at least not any time soon. Everybody knows that the corporate-conservative coalition and the Republican Party are extremely powerful in the United States. They usually can influence the government on decisions of interest to them through their hired lobbyists, public relation firms, expert testimony, campaign finance donations, and appointments to important governmental positions. Nothing new about any of that. The business of America is business. The name of the system is corporate capitalism.

Moreover, the great majority of people are currently willing to go along with this system, partly because they have a commitment to their everyday lives, which include a great many meaningful parts, such as family, work, religious observances, sports, hobbies, and community service, and partly because they currently cannot see anything they like better out there or a way to get from here to there even if they want something more. So they settle for the good things they have even while knowing that the social arrangements aren't fair.

But egalitarians of the past were up against the same problems, and they didn't ask for any guarantees. Everyone professes to see a clear pattern in history when they turn on their hindsight, but there is nothing inevitable about the future when it is looked at from the present. All the high-level theorists of the past decades, from elitists to mainstreamers to Marxists, proved to be dead wrong in their predictions. And the list of unexpected events runs long for the past one hundred years alone: World War I, the Bolshevik Revolution (even by Marxists), the Great Depression (especially by economists), the New Deal, the Chinese revolution, the civil rights movement, American defeat in Vietnam, the stock market crash of 1987 (especially by Reaganites), the collapse of the Soviet Union, majority rule in South Africa, the Persian Gulf War, the war in the Balkans, genocide in Rwanda, financial disasters in Mexico and Southeast Asia, the terrorist attacks in the United States on September 11, 2001, and the war on terrorism by the United States and its allies.

Rather clearly, humility is a virtue when it comes to talking about the future, although "futurists" of course make a nice living with their nonsense books and television babble. Nimbleness, flexibility, and patience are also necessary virtues. So is the ability to take risks when little openings occur due to unpredictable events ranging from nuclear plant accidents, oil spills, and corporate scandals to depressions and wars.

Despite all the failures and false starts that have been discussed in this book, egalitarians will have many unexpected opportunities to make their case over the next few decades. The purpose of this book has been to suggest the ways to make the most of those moments. It does not and could not provide detailed blueprints, but it does point to the pathways down which any specific actions would have to flow if egalitarian values are to be advanced when cracks and openings suddenly occur in the corporate power structure.

Egalitarians of America, unite. You can make a difference. I would not ask to be a consultant on your efforts if I thought otherwise.

ANNOTATED BIBLIOGRAPHY
AND SOURCE NOTES

Provided here are the citations for the quotes and facts that appear in the text. More generally, the citations are meant as starting points for further reading. They are a mix of the timely, topical, and accessible, along with what I find to be the clearest theoretical statements on given issues. These references are not meant to be exhaustive, and I apologize in advance to specialists in the many areas I have drawn on for not being able to provide a complete account of each of these literatures. Also provided here is the opportunity to make more detailed comments on a few issues. These comments are meant to deepen, extend, or nuance general claims in the text that would have bogged down the general flow of the narrative.

CHAPTER 1: THE WHAT-IF NADER CAMPAIGN OF 2000

Page 1. There is a good literature on comparative studies of electoral systems. For the most comprehensive studies, see Maurice Duverger, *Political parties,* 2nd ed. (New York: Wiley, 1959); Douglas W. Rae, *The political consequences of electoral laws,* rev. ed. (New Haven, Conn.: Yale University Press, 1971); and Seymour Martin Lipset and Gary Marks, *It didn't happen here: Why socialism failed in the United States* (New York: Norton, 2000), chapter 2.

Page 2. For the story of the Henry Wallace campaign, see James Weinstein, *Ambiguous legacy: The left in American politics* (New York: New Viewpoints, 1975), chapter 6; and Thomas W. Devine, "The eclipse of progressivism," (Ph.D. diss., University of North Carolina, Chapel Hill, 2000).

Page 3. For information on Upton Sinclair's End Poverty in California Campaign, see Greg Mitchell, *The campaign of the century: Upton Sinclair's race for governor of California and the birth of media politics* (New York: Random House, 1992).

Page 4. The hypothetical numbers at Nader rallies are based on the actual turnouts for his rallies as a Green Party candidate.

Page 5. The hypothetical claim that Nader started egalitarian Democratic clubs in forty-three states is based on the fact that he was on the ballot in forty-three states as the Green Party candidate.

Page 5. The hypothetical second- and third-level appointments in a Gore administration are based on the fact that several Nader colleagues were appointed to such positions by President Jimmy Carter.

Page 5. The hypothetical House seats that Nader saved from the Greens come from the fact that Greens did cost the Democrats House seats in Michigan and New Mexico, and almost in New Jersey.

Page 6. For good accounts of the problems of central planning and the possibilities of planning through the market, see Charles Lindblom, *Politics and markets: The world's political economic systems* (New York: Basic, 1977); Charles Lindblom, *The market system: What it is, how it works, and what to make of it* (New Haven, Conn.: Yale University Press, 2001); and Alex Nove, *The economics of feasible socialism revisited,* 2nd ed. (New York: HarperCollins, 1991).

Page 6. For an explanation of how a corporate-conservative coalition rooted in the ownership and control of large corporations dominates the weaker and more fragmented liberal-labor coalition, see G. William Domhoff, *Who rules America? Power and politics,* 4th ed. (New York: McGraw-Hill, 2002). In effect, *Who rules America?* provides the power context within which this current book on large-scale social change can be situated. Conversely, this current book can be read as a statement of the political analysis that follows from the sociological analysis in *Who rules America?*

Page 7. For the best accounts of strategic nonviolence, see Peter Ackerman and Christopher Kruegler, *Strategic nonviolent conflict: The dynamics of people power in the twentieth century* (Westport, Conn.: Praeger, 1994); Ronald M. McCarthy and Gene Sharp, *Nonviolent action: A research guide* (New York: Garland, 1997); and George Lakey, *Powerful peacemaking: A strategy for a living revolution* (Philadelphia: New Society Publishers, 1987).

Page 10. There are many classic justifications of hierarchy by conservatives throughout Western history. For one good brief summary of them, see T. B. Bottomore, *Elites and society* (London: Watts, 1964). For a modern-day equivalent in a right-wing book claiming African Americans are intellectually inferior, see Richard J. Herrnstein and Charles Murray, *The bell curve: Intelligence and class structure in American life* (New York: Free Press, 1994). For a thorough scholarly statement on the problem of dominators by social psychologists, as supported by their own research, see Jim Sidanius and Felicia Pratto, *Social dominance: An intergroup theory of social hierarchy and oppression* (New York: Cambridge University Press, 1999).

Page 10. For the importance of the liberal-conservative dimension in American politics, see Keith T. Poole and Howard Rosenthal, *Congress: A political-economic history of roll call voting* (New York: Oxford University Press, 1997).

Page 11. For an analysis of the "illiberal" tendencies within egalitarianism, see Richard J. Ellis, *The dark side of the left: Illiberal egalitarianism in America* (Lawrence: University Press of Kansas, 1998). The final pages of Ellis's book present the general outlines of a "liberal egalitarianism."

Page 11. For a discussion of how egalitarians can control tendencies toward elitism through defining themselves as catalysts and focusing on strategic nonviolence, see Richard Flacks, *Making history: The radical tradition in American life* (New York: Columbia University Press, 1988), 271–75. "Activists who choose a radical path and an elitist practice must begin their journey by refusing absolutely to reach for power, seeing instead that their mission is to serve as exemplars of moral being and action. They must refuse absolutely the belief that history can be short-circuited through violent intervention. They ought to study Thoreau, Tolstoy, Gandhi, Muste, and King as models of history making, rather than Lenin, Trotsky, Mao, Che, and Fanon" (275).

Page 13. For two sympathetic but critical studies of the history of the American left through the late 1960s and early 1970s, which show both its successes and failures, see Weinstein, *Ambiguous legacy;* and Flacks, *Making history,* chapter 4.

Page 13. For a summary of the living-wage campaign, see Jim Hightower, "Going down the road: Campaign for a living wage," *The Nation,* 1 April 2002, 8. For the early stages of the antisweatshop movement, see Randy Shaw, *Reclaiming America: Nike, clean air, and the new national activism* (Berkeley: University of California Press, 1999), chapters 1–2. For another account, see Marc Cooper, "No sweat: Uniting workers and students, a new movement is born," *The Nation,* 7 June 1999, 11–14.

CHAPTER 2: WHY EGALITARIANS SHOULD
TRANSFORM THE DEMOCRATIC PARTY

Page 17. The change in the party system in Belgium is discussed in Duverger, *Political parties,* 213, 220–21, 243–45.

Page 17. For the comparative studies of electoral systems, see Duverger, *Political parties;* Rae, *Political consequences of electoral laws;* and Lipset and Marks, *It didn't happen here,* chapter 2.

Page 18. For the best account of third parties in the United States, see Steven J. Rosenstone, Roy L. Behr, and Edward H. Lazarus, *Third parties in America:*

Citizen response to major party failure, 2nd ed. (Princeton, N.J.: Princeton University Press, 1996).

Page 18. For the meager representation of leftists in the U.S. Congress as compared to their representation in parliaments around the world, see Christopher Hewitt, "The effect of political democracy and social democracy on equality in industrial societies: A cross-national comparison," *American Sociological Review* 42, no. 3 (1977): 450–64. Two members of the Socialist Party were elected to Congress. Victor Berger was elected from the Milwaukee area in 1910, 1918, and 1922–1928; he died in office in 1929. Meyer London was elected from the lower east side of Manhattan in 1914, 1916, and 1920–1924. For details on the considerable success of the old Socialist Party in electoral politics at the local and state levels, see James Weinstein, *The decline of socialism in America: 1912–1925* (New York: Monthly Review, 1968). According to historian Harvey Klehr, *The heyday of American communism: The depression decade* (New York: Basic, 1984), 289–93, the following leftists in or close to the Communist Party were elected to the House in either 1936 or 1938: Jerry O'Connell of Montana, John Bernard of Minnesota, and Vito Marcantonio of New York. Two members from California also may have been close to the party. These leftists were one small part of a progressive block of about forty House members, most of them swept into office in 1936. However, over half of these progressives were gone after the 1938 elections—twenty-two lost their seats, three left on their own accord, and four failed in bids for the Senate. Marcantonio was elected in 1934 and in 1938–1950. In the early 1940s, Hugh DeLacy, a member of the Communist Party, was elected to Congress for one term from Washington State as a member of the Commonwealth Federation, a club within the Democratic Party of the kind advocated in this book. Since 1990, socialist Bernie Sanders of Vermont has been elected to the House as an independent.

Page 18. Technically speaking, the president is selected by the Electoral College, wherein each state casts its electoral votes for the candidate who received the most votes in that state. The focus on the electoral votes in each state forces candidates to concentrate on winning a plurality in as many states as possible, rather than simply on winning the most votes in the nation overall. This system creates a further disadvantage for third parties. However, abolishing the Electoral College would not make much difference as long as the winner did not have to receive a majority of the votes. See Rosenstone, Behr, and Lazarus, *Third parties in America,* 17–18.

Page 19. For a searing critique of the Constitution, see Robert A. Dahl, *How democratic is the American constitution?* (New Haven, Conn.: Yale University Press, 2002). Dahl does not see much change any time soon, but thinks the issue should be discussed.

Page 19. For a discussion about instant runoff voting, see Jim Hightower, "Let's go IRV," *The Nation,* 27 May 2002, 8. Its advocates have a website at www.fair vote.org (accessed August 2002).

Page 20. For the origins of primaries, see Allen F. Lovejoy, *La Follette and the establishment of the direct primary in Wisconsin, 1890–1904* (New Haven, Conn.: Yale University Press, 1941). For white primaries, see V. O. Key, *Southern politics in state and nation* (New York: Knopf, 1949). For an account of how a few socialists and the state's farmers took advantage of the primary system in North Dakota shortly before World War I, see the amazing history by Robert L. Morlan, *Political prairie fire: The nonpartisan league, 1915–1922* (St. Paul: Minnesota Historical Society Press, 1985).

Page 20. For an account of the insurgent campaign in the Democratic primaries by Estes Kefauver, see Charles L. Fontenay, *Estes Kefauver: A biography* (Knoxville: University of Tennessee Press, 1980). For the impact a little-known senator from Wisconsin had by running in the 1968 Democratic primaries as an antiwar candidate, see George Rising, *Clean for Gene: Eugene McCarthy's 1968 presidential campaign* (Westport, Conn.: Praeger, 1997).

Page 21. For a history of the Democratic Party from a power perspective, see G. William Domhoff, *The power elite and the state: How policy is made in America* (New York: Aldine de Gruyter, 1990), chapter 9. For the story of the reconstitution of the Democratic Party after the Civil War, see C. Vann Woodward, *Reunion and reaction: The compromise of 1877 and the end of reconstruction* (Boston: Little, Brown, 1966). For conservative control of the party in recent years, see Kenneth S. Baer, *Reinventing democrats: The politics of liberalism from Reagan to Clinton* (Lawrence: University Press of Kansas, 2000).

Page 21. For southern dominance of the party in the twentieth century and the role of the conservative voting bloc, see James T. Patterson, *Congressional conservatism and the new deal: The growth of the conservative coalition in Congress, 1933–1939* (Westport, Conn.: Greenwood, 1981); David M. Potter, *The South and the concurrent majority* (Baton Rouge: Louisiana State University Press, 1972); Mack C. Shelley II, *The permanent majority: The conservative coalition in the United States Congress* (Tuscaloosa: University of Alabama Press, 1983); and Lee J. Alston and Joseph P. Ferrie, *Southern paternalism and the American welfare state: Economics, politics, and institutions in the South, 1865–1965* (New York: Cambridge University Press, 1999). It needs to be emphasized that the conservative voting bloc was still forming on some issues into the 1990s, and usually won when it did form. For example, this is the coalition that passed the North Atlantic Free Trade Agreement.

Page 21. A "machine Democrat" was an elected official responsible to a tightly knit urban political organization, which usually was controlled by a highly autocratic leader. The machines were built on patronage to activists, such as government contracts and government jobs, along with favors to individual voters that made their everyday lives easier. Machines often used ethnic appeals to help keep newer immigrants aligned against more established Americans.

Page 21. On the origins of the National Labor Relations Board in a bargain between the liberal-labor coalition and the southern Democrats, a bargain that greatly upset the northern corporate elites of the time, see Domhoff, *Power elite and the state,* chapter 4.

Page 22. For an understanding of the machine Democrats, I draw on Norman C. Miller, "The machine Democrats," *Washington Monthly* (June 1970); Richard Bolling, *Power in the house* (New York: Dutton, 1968); and Martin Tolchin and Susan Tolchin, *To the victor . . .* (New York: Random House, 1971).

Page 22. For the trade-offs involved in the prospending alliance between the northern and southern Democrats, see Aage R. Clausen, *How congressmen decide* (New York: St. Martin's, 1973); and Michael K. Brown, *Race, money, and the American welfare state* (Ithaca, N.Y.: Cornell University Press, 1999).

Page 23. For the changes in the southern political economy that made the civil rights movement possible, see Jack M. Bloom, *Class, race, and the civil rights movement* (Bloomington: Indiana University Press, 1987).

Page 23. For an analysis of how the New Deal coalition came apart, see Edward G. Carmines and James A. Stimson, *Issue evolution: Race and the transformation of American politics* (Princeton, N.J.: Princeton University Press, 1989); and Domhoff, *Power elite and the state,* chapter 10.

Page 24. As the text implies, it is my view that no campaign finance reforms short of complete public financing of elections would have any significant effect. There are too many ways to beat most reforms, including the fact that a candidate's name recognition could be increased through financial support before he or she became a candidate. Eliminating all but small donations probably would not hurt the corporate-conservative coalition, although it might lead the coalition to favor candidates who are already well known, such as former generals like Dwight D. Eisenhower and former movie actors like Ronald Reagan. At the same time, as the American Civil Liberties Union suggests, limiting campaign finance may infringe on free speech. In addition, it may be riskier for small liberal or immigrant groups to lose their ability to raise large sums from a few individuals than it would be for the corporate-conservative coalition. Be that as it may, I do not think campaign finance is as critical as the reformers make it out to be. It is one piece of a larger picture. The bigger problems are the ones discussed in this book. For an excellent book on how campaign finance currently functions, and an argument for public financing of campaigns, see Dan Clawson, Alan Neustadtl, and Mark Weller, *Dollars and votes: How business campaign contributions subvert democracy* (Philadelphia: Temple University Press, 1998).

Page 26. See Ralph Nader, *Crashing the party* (New York: St. Martin's, 2002), 221, for his remark that "I always prefer to be a plaintiff rather than a defendant."

Page 27. John Lewis, *Walking with the wind: A memoir of the movement* (New York: Simon and Schuster, 1998) tells the moving story of his leadership in the civil rights movement and of his dramatic uphill battle for a seat in Congress.

Page 28. For the phrase "entrepreneurs of identity," see Bernd Simon and Bert

Klandermans, "Politicized collective identity," *American Psychologist* 56 (April 2001): 326.

Page 29. For the story of the 1986 campaign by insurgents in Michigan, see Dean Baker, "Left challenge on issues brings grassroots campaign gains," *In These Times*, 17–23 December 1986, 12.

Page 29. For the idea to run in a few very liberal districts, see James Weinstein, *The long detour* (Boulder, Colo.: Westview, 2003).

Page 29. Leftist readers with long historical memories may wonder how this strategy compares with the attempt by the Democratic Socialists of America to work within the Democratic Party in the 1970s. There are several major differences. The Democratic Socialists of America were so eager to be acceptable to liberals and organized labor that they went to the other extreme from the advocates of leftist third parties. They did not put forth their own candidates or develop a full program, but instead tried to help the most liberal of liberals while at the same time trying to support the cautious leaders of the AFL-CIO, a near-impossible stretch in itself. They thus were indistinguishable from liberals and restrained by their Marxian-derived belief in sticking close to organized labor as the clearest embodiment of the working class. They were unable to take any independent action, and therefore unable to challenge the party to take a new direction. They soon became invisible. For the story of the Democratic Socialists of America, see the autobiography and biography of one of its key founders, Michael Harrington. Michael Harrington, *The long-distance runner: An autobiography* (New York: Holt, 1988); and Maurice Isserman, *The other American: The life of Michael Harrington* (New York: Public Affairs Press, 2000).

Page 30. For the specifics on Jackson's vote totals in the South in 1988, see Frank Clemente and Frank Watkins, eds., *Keep hope alive: Jesse Jackson's 1988 presidential campaign* (Boston: South End, 1989), 233ff.

Page 32. See Nader, *Crashing the party*, 280, for the remark about Genghis Khan.

Page 32. See Nader, *Crashing the party*, 13, for the comment on the "liberal's archreactionary."

Page 33. See Nader, *Crashing the party*, 246, 307, for the claim that Democrats "anesthetize" activists. For the idea that the Democrats take activists for granted, see Nader, *Crashing the party*, 144.

Page 33. See Nader, *Crashing the party*, 204, for the claim that defeat is the only message that politicians understand.

Page 33. See Nader, *Crashing the party*, 207–8, for the claim that he was responsible for Maria Cantwell's senatorial victory in Washington State.

Page 34. For the growing differences between the two parties, see Poole and Rosenthal, *Congress*. For more recent information showing that the trend continues, see Richard E. Cohen, "A congress divided," *National Journal*, 5 February 2000, 382–404. For the best study of the current voting coalitions, see Jeff Manza and Clem Brooks, *Social cleavages and political change: Voter align-*

ments and U.S. party coalitions (New York: Oxford University Press, 1999). Manza and Brooks show that race, religion, and gender are better predictors of voting than social class as of the 1996 election. White men and women with less than a college education, who are the majority in the blue-collar working class, now vote in a majority for the Republicans.

Page 35. For an analysis of votes for H. Ross Perot in 1992, see Warren E. Miller and J. Merrill Shanks, *The new American voter* (Cambridge, Mass.: Harvard University Press, 1996).

Page 35. For the origins of the Social Security Act of 1935, see G. William Domhoff, *State autonomy or class dominance? Case studies on policy making in America* (New York: Aldine de Gruyter, 1996), chapter 5. For why the origins were lost from sight, see William Graebner, *A history of retirement: The meaning and function of an American institution, 1885–1978* (New Haven, Conn.: Yale University Press, 1980).

Page 35. See Nader, *Crashing the party*, 197–98, for the importance he gives to nonvoters. For evidence that nonvoters do not differ much in their political views from voters, see Raymond E. Wolfinger and Steven J. Rosenstone, *Who votes?* (New Haven, Conn.: Yale University Press, 1980). For a study showing the same thing for the 1980s by holding race, income, education, and age constant in voting statistics, see Ruy Teixeira, "What if we held an election and everybody came?" *American Enterprise* 3 (1992): 50–60. For more recent findings, see Ruy Teixeira, "Fool's gold of the left," *Dissent* 47 (2000): 45–49.

CHAPTER 3: MORE EQUALITY THROUGH THE MARKET SYSTEM

Page 39. I heard this remark at a talk by a well-known scholar-activist of the Marxian persuasion on a university campus in April 2001.

Page 40. For the classic attack on utopian socialism, see Friedrich Engels, *Socialism: Utopian and scientific* (New York: Scribner's, 1892).

Page 40. For the foundational texts concerning the Marxist view of history, showing what I think is a greater emphasis on the economic system than the political system within nation-states, see Karl Marx, "A contribution to the critique of political economy," in *The portable Karl Marx*, ed. Eugene Kamenka (New York: Penguin, 1983), 159–61; Karl Marx, "The German ideology," in *The portable Karl Marx*, ed. Eugene Kamenka (New York: Penguin, 1983), 163–71; and Karl Marx and Friedrich Engels, *The communist manifesto*, trans. Paul M. Sweezy (New York: Monthly Review, 1964). See also the accompanying essay by Paul Sweezy and Leo Huberman, "The Communist manifesto after 100 years."

Page 41. On the failures of central planning, see Nove, *Economics of feasible socialism revisited*, 91; and Lindblom, *Market system*. However, it should be added that there is a huge amount of literature on this topic that is only summarized in these books. Nove, for example, wrote many earlier books explicitly devoted to issues of central planning.

Page 41. For evidence that central planning was essential to Marx's view of socialism, see N. Scott Arnold, *Marx's radical critique of capitalist society: A reconstruction and critical evaluation* (New York: Oxford University Press, 1990), chapter 6. To understand why classical Marxists cannot consider the use of the market, see the analysis of the role of the market in Stanley Moore, *The critique of capitalist democracy: An introduction to the theory of the state in Marx, Engels, and Lenin* (New York: Kelley, 1969), chapter 2. For evidence that some of the most prominent Marxist scholars in the United States continue to see the market primarily in terms of deception, see Bertell Ollman, "Market mystification in capitalist and market socialist societies," in *Market socialism: The debate among socialists,* ed. Bertell Ollman (New York: Routledge, 1998). Ollman makes the following claim: "One major virtue of centrally planned societies, then, even undemocratic ones, even ones that don't work very well, is that it is easy to see who is responsible for what goes wrong. It is those who made the plan. The same cannot be said of market economies, which have as one of their main functions to befuddle the understanding of those who live in them. This is essential if people are to misdirect whatever frustration and anger they feel about the social and economic inequality, unemployment, idle machines and factories, ecological destruction, widespread corruption and exaggerated forms of greed that are the inevitable byproducts of market economies" (81). Ollman is not an extremist among Marxists on this issue.

Page 41. In the text, I say that capitalists realize a profit by selling goods on the market. Technically, however, profit comes out of the surplus value produced by workers and appropriated by capitalists, but capitalists do not sell surplus value. They sell commodities.

Page 42. For the quote from the editor of the *Socialist Register,* see Leo Panitch, *Renewing socialism: Democracy, strategy, and imagination* (Boulder, Colo.: Westview, 2001), 202.

Page 42. For good discussions of the possibilities of market socialism, see Nove, *Economics of feasible socialism revisited;* and Christopher Pierson, *Socialism after communism: The new market socialism* (Oxford: Polity, 1995). For the argument among Marxists about market socialism, see Ollman, *Market socialism.* The Marxists who advocate any form of market socialism, even in conjunction with a minimum of central planning or as a transitional program, are in the distinct minority in the general debate.

Page 42. For critiques of central planning, see Lindblom, *Market system;* and Nove, *Economics of feasible socialism.* For a dramatic statement of the failure of central planning in the Soviet Union, see Stephen Kotkin, *Magnetic mountain: Stalinism as a civilization* (Berkeley: University of California Press, 1995).

Page 43. For a friendly critique of market socialism that is skeptical about the workability of social ownership or any degree of central planning, see Pierson, *Socialism after communism*.

Page 43. For accessible accounts of the scholarly studies that upset the claims of those who attribute perfection to markets, see Paul Krugman, *Peddling prosperity: Economic sense and nonsense in the age of diminished expectations* (New York: Norton, 1994); and Robert Kuttner, *Everything for sale: The virtues and limits of markets* (New York: Knopf, 1997).

Page 43. For the argument that the market system could be even more efficient if there were greater equality, see Samuel Bowles and Herbert Gintis, *Recasting egalitarianism: New rules for communities, states, and markets* (New York: Verso, 1998).

Page 43. See Lindblom, *Market system*, chapter 18, for an excellent argument for the possibilities of planning through the market. No reader should reject the argument of this chapter out of hand without having read Lindblom very carefully.

Page 43. For information on this energy report, see David Moberg, "Fueling the flames," *In These Times*, 1 April 2002, 11–13. For the general case that environmental laws do not decrease the number of jobs, see Eban Goodstein, *The trade-off myth: Fact and fiction about jobs and the environment* (Washington, D.C.: Island, 1999).

Page 45. For a discussion of the limited rights actually needed by corporations in a market system, see Lindblom, *Market system*, 239.

Page 46. For one good account of the limits of the market in the domain of health care, see Kuttner, *Everything for sale*, chapter 4.

Page 46. For a good overview of the flexible use of markets in other countries, in some states in the United States, and during the New Deal, see Martin Carnoy and Derek Shearer, *Economic democracy: The challenge of the 1980s* (White Plains, N.Y.: Sharpe, 1980).

Page 47. On the high levels of job satisfaction over the past decades in the United States, see Richard F. Hamilton, *Marxism, revisionism, and Leninism: Explication, assessment, and commentary* (Westport, Conn.: Praeger, 2000), 124–25; and Richard F. Hamilton and James D. Wright, *The state of the masses* (New York: Aldine, 1986), chapter 6.

Page 47. For a good overall analysis of the earned income tax credit (EITC), see John Myles and Jill Quadagno, "Envisioning a third way: The welfare state in the twenty-first century," *Contemporary Sociology* 29, no. 1 (2000): 156–67. For the suggestion that a negative income tax should be used more widely than it is now, see Fred Block and Jeff Manza, "Could we end poverty in a postindustrial society?" *Politics and Society* 25 (1997): 473–512. For a model of an egalitarian market economy that incorporates the negative income tax, see Fred L. Block, *The vampire state* (New York: New Press, 1996), chapters 24–29. For another statement of what would be possible with the help of planning through the market and other government programs, see Benjamin Page and James R. Simmons, *What government could do: Dealing with poverty and inequality* (Chicago: University of Chicago Press, 2002). For information on the effectiveness of the current EITC system, see Robert Greenstein and Isaac Shapiro, *New research findings on the effects of the earned income tax credit* (Washington, D.C.: Center on Budget and Policy Priorities, 1998); and Bruce D. Meyer and Douglas Holtz-Eakin, eds., *Making work pay: The earned income tax credit and its impact on America's families* (New York: Russell Sage Foundation, 2001).

Page 48. For a good account of some of the policy possibilities within the context of a reconstructed market system, see Bowles and Gintis, *Recasting egalitarianism.*

CHAPTER 4: SOCIAL MOVEMENTS AND STRATEGIC NONVIOLENCE

Page 49. For a creative synthesis of the literature on the social psychology of social movements, based in part on his own original work, see Stephen C. Wright, "Strategic collective action: Social psychology and social change," in *Blackwell handbook of social psychology*, vol. 4, *Intergroup processes*, ed. Rupert Brown and Samuel L. Gaertner (Malden, Mass.: Blackwell, 2001).

Page 50. For the sentiment about "getting in the way of power" in a history of left activism from 1970 to 2000 by a longtime activist who describes herself as a "shut-it-down radical," see L. A. Kauffman, "Direct action: Radicalism in our time," *Free Radical*, no. 8 (July 2000), at www.free-radical.org (accessed August 2002).

Page 50. For a good account of strategic nonviolence, see Ackerman and Kruegler, *Strategic nonviolent conflict.*

Page 51. For the importance of African American churches in the civil rights movement, see Aldon Morris, *The origins of the civil rights movement: Black communities organizing for change* (New York: Free Press, 1984).

Page 52. Jerome Cohen, a lawyer for the United Farm Workers from 1967 to 1982, told me that Cesar Chavez repeatedly said violence is wrong and stupid.

Page 52. For an analysis of how violence contributed to the changes in American politics after 1965, see Thomas Byrne Edsall with Mary D. Edsall, *Chain reaction: The impact of race, rights, and taxes on American politics* (New York: Norton, 1991). For systematic information from polls, see Benjamin Page and Robert Y. Shapiro, *The rational public: Fifty years of trends in Americans' policy preferences* (Chicago: University of Chicago Press, 1992), 90–94.

Page 52. The most famous example of the point concerning the public's reaction to violence toward the police concerns the police riot in Chicago at the time of the Democratic National Convention in 1968. As the police attacked, the demonstrators chanted "the whole world is watching" because they thought people would see that the police were at fault. Instead, polls showed that a majority of people sided with the police. See Todd Gitlin, *The whole world is watching: Mass media in the making and unmaking of the New Left* (Berkeley: University of California Press, 1980).

Page 53. The questions that should be raised by practitioners of strategic nonviolence come from Ackerman and Kruegler, *Strategic nonviolent conflict*, chapter 2.

Page 53. For an analysis of the politics of the civil rights movement, see Doug McAdam, *Political process and the development of black insurgency, 1930–1970*, 2nd ed. (Chicago: University of Chicago Press, 1999).

Page 54. For an outstanding book on the strategy of outing and how it developed, see Larry Gross, *Contested closets: The politics and ethics of outing* (Minneapolis: University of Minnesota Press, 1993). The book makes several comparisons with the civil rights movement.

Page 55. For the outing of Congressman Jim Kolbe of Arizona, see David W. Dunlap, "A republican congressman discloses he is a homosexual," *New York Times*, 3 August 1996, 1. For a discussion of gays and lesbians in the political elite, see Richard L. Zweigenhaft and G. William Domhoff, *Diversity in the power elite: Have women and minorities reached the top?* (New Haven, Conn.: Yale University Press, 1998), 166–73.

Page 55. For a journalistic account of the AIDS Coalition to Unleash Power and its successes, see Jason DePerle, "Rude, rash, and effective," *New York Times*, 3 January 1990, A12. For an excellent scholarly analysis, see Joshua Gamson, "Silence, death, and the invisible enemy: AIDS activism and social movement 'newness,'" *Social Problems* 38 (1989): 351–67. For documents relating to the history of ACT UP, see www.actupny.org/documents/documents.html (accessed August 2002).

Page 56. For a descriptive account of left activism between 1964 and 1969, based in large part on interviews with key participants, see Lawrence Lader, *Power on the left: American radical movements since 1946* (New York: Norton, 1979), chapters 12–18. For a moving account of events from 1964 through 1966 by a young white liberal who became very disenchanted with the United States, see Paul Cowan, *The making of an un-American: A dialogue with experience* (New York: Viking, 1970). For an excellent discussion of how the focus on nonviolence was lost, see Nigel Young, *An infantile disorder? The crisis and decline of the new left* (Boulder, Colo.: Westview, 1977), chapter 12.

Page 56. For one fine account of the evolution of the Student Nonviolent Coordinating Committee, see Clayborne Carson, *In struggle: SNCC and the black awakening of the 1960s* (Cambridge, Mass.: Harvard University Press, 1995). For the perspective of an activist who wanted to stay with nonviolence, see Lewis, *Walking with the wind*. For the perspective of one of those who opposed the continuation of nonviolence and thought of himself as a revolutionary, see

James Forman, *The making of black revolutionaries,* 2nd ed. (Washington, D.C.: Open Hand, 1985). For an excellent overview of the black uprisings as a whole, see James A. Geschwender, ed., *The black revolt: The civil rights movement, ghetto uprisings, and separatism* (Englewood Cliffs, N.J.: Prentice-Hall, 1971).

Page 58. For evidence of poll changes after violence, see Page and Shapiro, *Rational public,* 90–94.

Page 58. For an account of the antiwar movement from the point of view of the young activists in Students for a Democratic Society (SDS), see James Miller, *Democracy is in the streets: From Port Huron to the siege of Chicago* (Cambridge, Mass.: Harvard University Press, 1994). For an earlier account of SDS, see Kirkpatrick Sale, *SDS: Ten years toward a revolution* (New York: Random House, 1973). For one former SDS leader's reflections on the left wing of the antiwar movement and how it gradually embraced violence, and thereby isolated itself from nonviolent liberals and moderates, see Todd Gitlin, *The sixties: Years of hope, days of rage* (New York: Bantam, 1987). For the unexpected fact that "as the war steadily lost popularity in the late Sixties, so did the anti-war movement," see Gitlin, *Sixties,* 262. For the deepest and most sobering analysis of how SDS moved toward violence, see Ellis, *Dark side of the left,* chapters 4–5.

Page 59. For useful articles on the global justice movement by members and supporters of it, see Eddie Yuen, George Katsiaficas, and Daniel Burton Rose, eds., *The battle of Seattle: The new challenge to capitalist globalization* (New York: Soft Skull, 2001). For another excellent account of the global justice movement by one of its leading journalists-activists, see the nineteen columns by L. A. Kauffman, *Free Radical,* at www.free-radical.org. See especially her history of the movement since 1994, "Back story," *Free Radical,* no. 10 (September 2000).

Page 60. For an excellent account of the "Battle for Seattle," including the comment about the broken windows, see Marc Cooper, "Street fight in Seattle," *The Nation,* 20 December 1999, 3–4.

Page 60. For the story of the demonstrations in Quebec City in May 2000, I relied on David Moberg, "Tear down the walls," *In These Times,* 28 May 2001, 11–14; Abby Scher, "A diversity of tactics?" *In These Times,* 28 May 2001, 16–17; and David Graeber, "Wall done," *In These Times,* 28 May 2001, 17. The quotes from Howl are in the article by Scher.

Page 61. For the second thoughts about property destruction and battling with the police, see Marc Cooper, "From protest to politics: A report from Porto Alegre," *The Nation,* 11 March 2002, 11–15.

Page 62. For how those who advocate strategic nonviolence would maintain nonviolent discipline and deal with those who foment violence, see Ackerman and Kruegler, *Strategic nonviolent conflict,* 42–45.

Page 62. For the sentiment by movement activists that violent tactics are no longer appropriate for the global justice movement in the light of the attacks on September 11, 2001, see Eddie Yuen, introduction to *The battle of Seattle: The new challenge to capitalist globalization,* ed. Eddie Yuen, George Katsiaficas, and Daniel Burton Rose (New York: Soft Skull, 2001); and the column by longtime activist and movement historian L. A. Kauffman, "All has changed," *Free Radical,* no. 19 (17 September 2001), at www.free-radical.org.

CHAPTER 5: REDEFINING WHO'S US AND WHO'S THEM

Page 63. The typical scenario for rightists and leftists is taken from Chip Berlet and Matthew N. Lyons, *Right-wing populism in America: Too close for comfort* (New York: Guilford, 2000). The authors applied the analysis only to the right in the book just cited, but they are now working on a manuscript that suggests that it applies to some organizations on the left as well.

Page 64. For the latest findings on the wealth and income distributions, see Edward N. Wolff, *Top heavy: The increasing inequality of wealth in America and what can be done about it,* 2nd ed. (New York: New Press, 2002).

Page 64. For information on inheritance, see Laurence Kotlikoff and Jagadeesh Gokhale, *The baby boomers' mega-inheritance: Myth or reality?* (Cleveland, Ohio: Federal Reserve Bank of Cleveland, 2000). For the latest on the income distribution, see Alan B. Krueger, "Economic scene," *New York Times,* 4 April 2002, C2; and Thomas Piketty and Emmanuel Saez, "Income inequality in the United States, 1913–1998," National Bureau of Economic Research, at www .nber.org (accessed August 2002).

Page 64. For a detailed account of how the top executives and stockholders of large corporations dominate the U.S. government through a corporate-conservative coalition that operates increasingly through the Republican Party, but still maintains strong influence in the presidential wing of the Democratic Party, see Domhoff, *Who rules America?*

Page 65. For the ideas and strategies of American Marxists in the 1870s, see Paul Buhle, *Marxism in the United States: Remapping the history of the American left* (London: Verso, 1987), chapter 1.

Page 66. For the long-standing nature of the American rejection of class, see Jackson Turner Main, *The social structure of revolutionary America* (Princeton, N.J.: Princeton University Press, 1965).

Page 67. For an analysis of the open-ended strategy of the civil rights movement based on social psychology, see Anthony R. Pratkanis and Marlene Turner, "Nine principles of successful affirmative action: Mr. Branch Rickey, Mr. Jackie Robinson, and the integration of baseball," *Nine: A Journal of Baseball History and Social Policy Perspectives* 3 (1994): 36–65.

Page 67. For an excellent analysis of the social psychology of social change, see Wright, "Strategic collective action." One of the virtues of Wright's analysis is that it also discusses the social psychology of why collective action is so rare despite glaring inequalities and injustices. On the social psychology of collective political action, see also Simon and Klandermans, "Collectivized political identity."

Page 68. For the figures on party identification, see Harris Poll, no. 8 (13 February 2002), at www.harrisinteractive.com/harris_poll/index.asp?PID = 285 (accessed August 2002). Using a slightly different approach, the National Election Survey conducted by social scientists at the University of Michigan reports that 50 percent say they are Democrats if independents who "lean" toward the Democrats are included, whereas 37 percent are Republicans if leaners are counted, and only 12 percent are independents. For the National Election Survey results, see www.umich.edu/~nes/nesguide/toptable/tab2a_2.htm (accessed August 2002). For the figures on liberals, moderates, and conservatives, see the Harris Poll, no. 8 (13 February 2002). For the slightly different finding that 29 percent are conservatives, 50 percent moderates, and 20 percent liberals according to exit polls after the 2000 election, and for a good overall portrait of American voters over the past three decades, see Marjorie Connelly, "Who voted: A portrait of American politics, 1976–2000," New York Times, 12 November 2000, 4.

Page 69. For George Soros's views, see George Soros, On globalization (New York: Public Affairs, 2002). For a review by a Nobel Prize–winning economist that endorses much of what Soros suggests, see Joseph E. Stiglitz, "A fair deal for the world," New York Review, 23 May 2002, 24–28. For Stiglitz's views on how globalization could be carried out in a humane manner, see Joseph E. Stiglitz, Globalization and its discontents (New York: New Press, 2002).

Page 70. For Jon Corzine's views, see Jon Corzine, "A time to be bold," The Nation, 16 April 2001, 6–7. He wrote this article to explain why he declined to join the Democratic Leadership Council. For a systematic study of how a small number of wealthy young adults have found a way to work for progressive change through philanthropy, see Susan A. Ostrander, Money for change: Social movement philanthropy at Haymarket People's Fund (Philadelphia: Temple University Press, 1995). Ostrander's study is clear evidence that all members of the capitalist class are not opponents of egalitarian social change.

CHAPTER 6: KEEPING LEADERS ACCOUNTABLE

Page 71. For the new and interesting idea that hunting and gathering societies had both group-level sharing and inverted power structures, see Christopher Boehm, Hierarchy in the forest: The evolution of egalitarian behavior (Cambridge, Mass.: Harvard University Press, 1999).

Page 72. For an analysis of the resistance to the rise of power structures and their eventual rise in five or six places in the past five thousand years, see the important book by Michael Mann, *The sources of social power,* vol. 1 (New York: Cambridge University Press, 1986), chapters 2–3.

Page 72. For the classic statement of the Iron Law of Oligarchy, see Robert Michels, *Political parties: A sociological study of the oligarchical tendencies of modern democracy* (Glencoe, Ill.: Free Press, 1915). For modern statements of the inevitability of elites within organizations for organizational reasons, not genetic or psychological ones, see John Higley and G. Lowell Fields, *Elitism* (Boston: Routledge and Kegan Paul, 1980); John Higley and Gyorgy Lengyel, eds., *Elites after state socialism: Theories and analysis* (Lanham, Md.: Rowman & Littlefield, 2000); and in a short and very accessible form, Michael Burton and John Higley, "Invitation to elite theory: The basic contentions," in *Power elites and organizations,* ed. G. William Domhoff and Thomas R. Dye (Beverly Hills, Calif.: Sage, 1987).

Page 73. For the problems in the United Farm Workers, see Theo J. Majka and Linda C. Majka, "Decline of the farm labor movement in California: Organizational crisis and political change," *Critical Sociology* 19 (1992): 3–36. For a public statement of Chavez's failings by one of his former lawyers, see Jerome Cohen, "UFW must get back to organizing," *Los Angeles Times,* 15 January 1986, 5. Cohen notes that Chavez blames the conservative Republican governor who was elected in 1982 for his problems, but then writes that "[a]s farm labor election statistics prove, the union stopped organizing effectively before Dukmejian became governor in 1982. . . . [H]ere we should render unto Cesar what is Cesar's, namely, the responsibility for the UFW's failure as yet to fulfill its promise." My account also builds on conversations with Cohen, and also with William H. Friedland, one of the leading experts on farm workers in the United States. For further evidence, see Frank Bardacke, "Cesar's ghost: Decline and fall of the U.F.W.," *The Nation,* 26 July 1993, 130–35.

Page 74. For the voting figures from the 1984 and 1988 campaigns, see Clemente and Watkins, *Keep hope alive,* 233ff. For comments on the limitations of Jesse Jackson and his 1984 campaign, see Manning Marable, "Jackson and the Rise of the Rainbow," *New Left Review* 149 (1985): 3–44; and Sheila D. Collins, *The rainbow challenge: The Jackson campaign and the future of U.S. politics* (New York: Monthly Review, 1986). For an account of the chaotic 1988 campaign, which shows Jackson's need to monopolize all media appearances, and to denigrate any staff members who have connections outside the campaign, see the analysis by journalist Elizabeth O. Colton, his former press secretary, *The Jackson phenomenon* (New York: Doubleday, 1989). On the lack of organization in his Rainbow Coalition, see Jamin B. Raskin, "Rainbow signs," *The Nation,* 1 July 1991, 4–6. For evidence that Jackson did not do a good job of building organizations because of the conflict between his charismatic style and the needs of an organization, see the balanced account by Ernest R. House, *Jesse Jackson and the politics of charisma: The rise and fall of the PUSH/Excel program* (Boulder,

Colo.: Westview, 1988), chapters 10, 11, 13. For a good description of Jackson's life and career, see Marshall Frady, *Jesse: The life and pilgrimage of Jesse Jackson* (New York: Random House, 1996).

Page 75. For the story of the Democratic Workers Party, see Janja Lalich, "A little carrot and a lot of stick: A case example," in *Recovery from cults,* ed. Michael D. Langone (New York: Norton, 1993), 51–84. For the best general overview on cults from a sociological point of view, see Mary Beth Ayella, *Insane therapy: Portrait of a psychotherapy cult* (Philadelphia: Temple University Press, 1998), chapters 1, 8. For an analysis of how seemingly leaderless egalitarian organizations come to be dominated by charismatic leaders, see Ellis, *Dark side of the left,* chapter 6; and Jo Freeman, "The tyranny of structurelessness," *Berkeley Journal of Sociology* 17 (1972–1973): 151–64.

Page 76. See Nader, *Crashing the party,* 57–58, for the list of colleagues that Nader criticizes for refusing to join him and for the claim that they would have supported him if he ran as a Democrat.

Page 77. For the story about the Nader aide who said the goal was to punish Gore, I relied on the first-person account by Harry Levine, an outstanding sociologist. See his assertion that Nader was out to sink Gore at www.hereinstead.com (accessed August 2002).

Page 77. The citation on the newspaper interview with Nader in the spring of 2001 is Dick Polman, "An unrepentant Nader sticks to his plan," *Philadelphia Inquirer,* 4 March 2001, A1.

Page 80. To understand why the role of unions in the liberal-labor coalition is so complex, see William Form, *Divided we stand: Working-class stratification in America* (Urbana: University of Illinois Press, 1985); and William Form, *Segmented labor, fractured politics: Labor politics in American life* (New York: Plenum, 1995). For a critique of most unions as not doing a good enough job of organizing, see Kate Bronfenbrenner, "Changing to organize: Unions know what has to be done," *The Nation,* 3 September 2001, 16–19. For a somewhat different view of the problems facing unions, see the reply by Nelson Lichtenstein, "Reply to Bronfenbrenner," *The Nation,* 3 September 2001, 29.

Page 80. To understand the necessity of government protection in order to make unionization possible, see Kim Voss, *The making of American exceptionalism: The Knights of Labor and class formation in the nineteenth century* (Ithaca, N.Y.: Cornell University Press, 1993); and Sidney Fine, *Sit-down: The General Motors strike of 1936–1937* (Ann Arbor: University of Michigan Press, 1969). See also the analysis and references in Domhoff, *Power elite and the state,* chapter 4.

Page 80. For the extent of union donations to the Democratic Party, see the valuable online compilation by the Center for Responsive Politics at www.crp.org (accessed August 2002).

Page 81. For an account of the living-wage campaigns, see Hightower, "Going down the road." For the antisweatshop movement, see Shaw, *Reclaiming America*. But for organizational conflicts in the antisweatshop movement, see Liza Featherstone, "The student movement comes of age," *The Nation*, 16 October 2000, 23–25.

Page 81. For the organizational structure of the feminist movement, one excellent source is Ruth Rosen, *The world split open: How the modern women's movement changed America* (New York: Viking, 2000). I do not want to imply that there were no tensions within and among these organizations, but my stress here is on the general network structure. For a discussion of the origins and tensions in this network, see Jo Freeman, "The origins of the women's liberation movement," *American Journal of Sociology* 78 (1973): 792–811.

Page 82. For the problems of invisible hierarchy in the global justice movement, see Yuen, introduction to *The battle of Seattle*, 10. See also Stephanie Guilloud, "Spark, fire, and burning coals: An organizer's history of Seattle," in *The battle of Seattle: The new challenge to capitalist globalization*, ed. Eddie Yuen, George Katsiaficas, and Daniel Burton Rose (New York: Soft Skull, 2001). In this context, it is also useful to recall Freeman, "Tyranny of structurelessness." Freeman points out that a lack of formal organizational structure can become a way of masking power, which can be all the more arbitrary because of the claim that it is not being exercised. This is why formal controls on leadership are essential to a "liberal egalitarianism," as stressed by Ellis, *Dark side of the left*.

Page 83. For the role of revolutionary Marxists from the Trotskyist International Socialist Organization in the antiwar protests of 2002, see Liza Featherstone, "The mideast war breaks out on campus," *The Nation*, 17 June 2002, 18–21. For a comment on the role of the Stalinist Workers World Party in the global justice movement, see Kauffman, "All has changed."

CHAPTER 7: A NEW FOREIGN POLICY AND A NEW STANCE ON RELIGION

Page 87. For the evidence that Marxists put the greatest weight on the economic base in the power equation, see Marx, "Contribution to the critique of political economy," 159–61; and Marx, "German ideology," 163–71.

Page 88. For Vladimir Lenin on imperialism, see V. I. Lenin, *Imperialism: The highest stage of capitalism* (New York: International, 1933). Lenin's view, with slight updates, was incorporated into most versions of Marxism, including the versions of Marxism that I am critiquing in this chapter.

Page 88. The story of the Americans who visited new communist countries is drawn from the work of Paul Hollander, *Political pilgrims: Western intellectuals in search of the good society*, 4th ed. (New Brunswick, N.J.: Transaction, 1998).

Page 88. On the grassroots work of the American Communist Party in the 1930s, see Flacks, *Making history*, 128–31, 143–60; and Mark Naison, *Communists in Harlem during the depression* (Urbana: University of Illinois Press, 1983).

Page 89. For an excellent brief account of the role of the Communist Party in the Congress of Industrial Organizations, see Weinstein, *Ambiguous legacy*, chapter 3.

Page 89. For an account of the Communist Party role in the Henry Wallace campaign, see Weinstein, *Ambiguous legacy*, chapter 6, and especially Devine, "The eclipse of progressivism."

Page 90. For the claim that he and other SDS leaders "slid into romance with the other side," see Gitlin, *Sixties*, 261. For the admission by one of the people who went to Hanoi in 1965 that he had been "snookered," see Gitlin, *Sixties*, 267. More generally, Gitlin, *Sixties*, chapter 11, provides an extremely compelling account of how SDS and the rest of the New Left became anti-American and pro-Hanoi/National Liberation Front. His book is a case study in how not to build a large-scale egalitarian movement.

Page 91. The main revolutionary Marxist groups that are still active in the antiwar and global justice movements are the International Socialist Organization and the Workers World Party.

Page 91. The rest of this chapter is indebted for its overall framework to the highly original synthesis of work on international power and economics by Michael Mann, *Global civil wars* (unpublished manuscript). This work in turn is based on his creative new theory of power that is being utilized to explore the sources of power in Western civilization from its very beginnings to the late twentieth century in his magisterial work *The sources of social power*, 3 vols. (New York: Cambridge University Press, 1986, 1993, and forthcoming).

Page 92. For the quote from Condoleezza Rice warning the Venezuelan president to "respect constitutional processes," see Paul Krugman, "Losing Latin America," *New York Times*, 16 April 2002, A31. For the first story of American involvement, see Christopher Marquis, "Bush officials met with Venezuelans who ousted leader," *New York Times*, 16 April 2002, A1.

Page 93. For the tragic misuse of elections for ethnic cleansing, see Michael Mann, "The dark side of democracy: The modern tradition of ethnic and political cleansing," *New Left Review* 235 (May–June 1999): 18–20.

Page 93. The comment about the need to manage transitions comes from Larry Diamond, as quoted in Thomas L. Friedman, "The free-speech bind," *New York Times*, 27 March 2002, A23. For Diamond's views on democracy, see Larry Diamond and Marc F. Plattner, *Developing democracy: Toward consolidation* (Baltimore, Md.: Johns Hopkins University Press, 1999); and Larry Diamond and Marc F. Plattner, eds., *The global divergence of democracies* (Baltimore, Md.: Johns Hopkins University Press, 2001).

Page 93. For a good account of the role of American activists in the antiapartheid struggle, see Donald R. Culverson, *Contesting apartheid: U.S. activism, 1960–1987* (Boulder, Colo.: Westview, 1999).

Page 93. The estimate that one-third of the major global disputes in the world today involve the quest for nation-states on the part of oppressed peoples is drawn from Mann, *Global civil wars.*

Page 94. For the quotation from Clinton concerning unilateral action, see Noam Chomsky, *9–11* (New York: Seven Stories, 2001), 111.

Page 94. The specifics of a Palestinian–Israeli compromise come from the text of a full-page ad that left and liberal American Jews ran. See *New York Times,* 17 July 2002, A21.

Page 94. For Jimmy Carter's views on solving the Palestinian–Israeli conflict, see Jimmy Carter, "America can persuade Israel to make a just peace," *New York Times,* 21 April 2002, 13.

Page 95. For several examples of covert actions against other nations by the United States since the early 1980s, see Chomsky, *9–11.* Chomsky also notes that the United States was found guilty of unlawful interference in another nation by the World Court in 1986 on the basis of evidence that it was funding the terrorism against civilian targets in Nicaragua by the contras.

Page 96. For the fact that the United States gives only 0.1 percent of its gross domestic product in foreign aid, the lowest figure for thirty wealthy nations, see Jeff Madrick, "Economic scene," *New York Times,* 1 November 2001, C2. The Netherlands is the highest at 0.79 percent, and France gives 0.39 percent. For a detailed popular account of this issue, see John Cassidy, "Helping hands: How foreign aid could help everybody," *New Yorker,* 18 March 2002, 60–66.

Page 96. For an account that synthesizes and adds to the critique of the destructive free trade regime sponsored by the United States, see Block, *Vampire state,* chapters 20–23. For his suggestions on how an egalitarian market economy should deal with these issues, see Block, *Vampire state,* 249–51, 266–68. The American emphasis on free trade is made all the more objectionable by the fact that the United States does not practice it in terms of agriculture, textiles, or steel for political reasons.

Page 97. For a discussion of the ways in which religious images and identities are often incorporated into social movements, see Ronald R. Aminzade and Elizabeth J. Perry, "The sacred, religious, and secular in contentious politics: Blurring boundaries," in *Silence and voice in the study of contentious politics,* ed. Ronald R. Aminzade et al. (New York: Cambridge University Press, 2001).

Page 97. Freeman Dyson, "Science and religion: No end in sight," *New York Review of Books* 49 (28 March 2002): 4–5.

Page 98. For the ways in which the Catholic Church nurtured the antiabortion movement, see Dallas A. Blanchard, *The anti-abortion movement and the rise of the religious right: From polite to fiery protest* (New York: Twayne, 1994); and Steve Askin, *A new rite: Conservative Catholic organizations and their allies* (Washington, D.C.: Catholics for a Free Choice, 1994).

CHAPTER 8: STOP BLAMING THE MEDIA

Page 99. See Nader, *Crashing the party*, 10, 12, for his comments concerning the media's influence on violence and the nature of the interactions of protestors with police.

Page 100. For his sustained attack on the Commission on Presidential Debates, see Nader, *Crashing the party*, 58–59, 63, 158–61, 220–39, 295. Nader sued the commission for barring him from attending the debate in Boston, even as a mere spectator who had a ticket. In April 2002, Nader settled the lawsuit when the commission agreed to issue an apology and pay an undisclosed amount of money just as the suit was about to go to trial.

Page 100. For information on media concentration, see Ben H. Bagdikian, *The media monopoly*, 6th ed. (Boston: Beacon, 2000). For the classic left statement on the media, see the propaganda model in Edward S. Herman and Noam Chomsky, *Manufacturing consent: The political economy of the mass media* (New York: Pantheon, 1988). For a critique of the model, see Jeff Goodwin, "What's right (and wrong) about left media criticism? Herman and Chomsky's propaganda model," *Sociological Forum* 9 (1994): 101–11. For the limitations of the model in the case of public opinion concerning the North Atlantic Free Trade Agreement, where union affiliation and critical awareness of the issues played a greater role, see Suzanne M. Coshow, "Media influence of public opinion on NAFTA" (paper presented at the annual meeting of the Pacific Sociological Association, San Francisco, 16–19 April 1998).

Page 100. For the study of chain newspapers, see David P. Demers, *The menace of the corporate newspaper: Fact or fiction?* (Ames: Iowa State University Press, 1996).

Page 101. For the differences of opinion between media and corporations, see Allen H. Barton, "Fault lines in American elite consensus," *Daedalus* (1980); Allen H. Barton, "Background, attitudes, and activities of American elites," *Research in Politics and Society* 1 (1985): 173–218; and Herbert Gans, "Are U.S. journalists dangerously liberal?" *Columbia Journalism Review* (November–December 1985): 29–33.

Page 101. For experimental studies of agenda setting based on the viewing of television news in laboratory settings, see Shanto Kyengar and Adam F. Simon, "New perspectives and evidence on political communication and campaign effects," *Annual Review of Psychology* 51 (2000): 149–62.

Page 101. For a summary of studies suggesting that television news probably does not have much impact in the real world, see Robert Erikcson and Kent Tedin, *American public opinion*, 5th ed. (Boston: Allyn and Bacon, 1995).

Page 102. For evidence that people screen out media information that does not fit their general frameworks, see William A. Gamson, *Talking politics* (New York: Cambridge University Press, 1992).

Page 102. On the impact of crime news, see L. Heath and K. Gilbert, "Mass media and fear of crime," *American Behavioral Scientist* 39 (1996): 379–86.

Page 102. For the claim that the Bill Clinton impeachment campaign may have increased resentment toward the media, see William Schneider, "And lo, the momentum shifted," *National Journal,* 3 October 1998, 2350.

Page 103. For empirical studies on the crucial issue of how the news is produced, see Gaye Tuchman, *Making news: A study in the construction of reality* (New York: Free Press, 1978); Herbert J. Gans, *Deciding what's news: A study of CBS evening news, NBC nightly news, Newsweek, and Time* (New York: Pantheon, 1979); and Michael Schudson, *The power of news* (Cambridge, Mass.: Harvard University Press, 1995). These books show that journalists have a fair degree of autonomy as professionals who respect the values and traditions of independent news gathering within which they work.

Page 103. For evidence on how useful the media have been in the antisweatshop movement, see Shaw, *Reclaiming America,* chapters 1–2.

CHAPTER 9: MAKING THE FUTURE YOURS

Page 105. For the historical successes and failures of the left, see Weinstein, *Ambiguous legacy;* and Flacks, *Making history,* chapter 4.

Page 108. Concerning the point that the great majority go along with the system, it is very important to grasp theoretically what most of us observe every day. Most people have a commitment to their everyday lives, which means that they do not stop their lives and make history unless they have to. Contrary to the conclusions put forth by unnecessarily abstract theorists of consciousness, who try to explain away left failures by claiming people have "false consciousness" due to the power of capitalists, people are not deceived about their social situations. Instead, I believe they have chosen to live their lives as best they can. This crucial point is a great frustration to activists, who have decided that their everyday lives will be dedicated to making history. For the dramatic differences between the lives of everyday people and activists, see Jack Whalen and Richard Flacks, *Beyond the barricades: The sixties generation grows up* (Philadelphia: Temple University Press, 1989). For theoretical challenges to those who stress false consciousness, see, Michael Mann, "The ideology of intellectuals and other people in the development of capitalism," in *Stress and contradiction in modern capitalism,* ed. Leon N. Lindberg et al. (Lexington, Mass.: Lexington, 1975); and Flacks, *Making history,* especially 23–24.

ACKNOWLEDGMENTS

I want to thank several people whose comments greatly improved this book in both tone and substance. I hope their willingness to help a heretic does not compromise their good standing in the academic and political circles to which they belong. First, I want to thank Rhonda F. Levine for her support and encouragement while reading several versions of the manuscript from start to finish, all the while providing extremely valuable theoretical and editorial suggestions.

I also want to thank Fred L. Block, Michael Mann, and Harvey Molotch for reading the penultimate draft and making suggestions that led to numerous changes. In addition, I am grateful to Richard J. Ellis for reading the entire manuscript and providing reassurances on several issues. I also thank all of them for very useful published work, which has shaped my thinking over the past several years.

Dick Flacks provided frank and helpful feedback on earlier versions of the sections on markets and foreign policy. Steve Wright provided me with many insights on the social psychology of social movements. Jim Weinstein answered numerous historical questions that I posed to him. I also drew extensively on the fine published work of these three colleagues in formulating my thoughts.

Dean Birkenkamp, my editor on this book, gave me an early and reassuring reading along with several comments that led me to change or sharpen my argument on several points. Joel Domhoff, journalist and writing instructor par excellence, improved the readability of the book with many good editorial suggestions relating to my tendency to become a little too academic at times.

I don't think I could have done it without all this help. At the least, it would have been a much less readable and coherent effort.

When I sat down to write, I expressed my hesitations to Michael Mann about risking such an endeavor. He sent me the following e-mail message that I kept on my iMac while I wrote: "You really ought to write your book on the left. If it concerns your friends, just don't be polemical, take their views seriously and sympathetically, and then criticize them." I hope I have been able to meet that standard.

INDEX

abortion, 98
ACORN (Association of Community Organizations for Reform), 81
action, collective, 123
activists, 8, 26, 103; antiwar, 58–59; commonalities, 12; Democratic Party and, 32–33; egalitarian (*see* egalitarians); everyday people and, 99, 130; recruiting, 31; results gained, 40; role of, 49
ACT UP (AIDS Coalition to Unleash Power), 55–56
AFL (American Federation of Labor), 89
AFL-CIO (American Federation of Labor and Congress of Industrial Organizations), 80, 81
African Americans: as candidates, 29–30; disenfranchisement of, 20, 22; government support for, 56
AIDS, 55–56
AIDS Coalition to Unleash Power (ACT UP), 55–56
allies, 22; attracting, 4, 52, 53; becoming enemies, 69; liberals as, 62
American Federation of Labor (AFL), 89
American Federation of Labor and

Congress of Industrial Organizations (AFL-CIO), 80, 81
Anderson, John, 33, 35
anti-Americanism, 85–86
anti-imperialism, 85–86, 87, 90–91; economic imperialism, 95–96
antisweatshop campaign, 13, 80–81
antiwar movements, 58–59, 90–91; Marxists in, 91, 127
apartheid, 14
assembly, freedom of, 10
Association of Community Organizations for Reform (ACORN), 81

Belgium, 17
Berger, Victor, 112
Bernard, John, 112
Black Panthers, 56, 57
blueprints, 39–40
Bolshevik Revolution, 86, 87
bourgeoisie, petite, 63, 65
boycotts, 53–54
Bradley, Bill, 3
Buchanan, Patrick, 19, 55
Bush, George W., 19, 32, 34; as corporate-conservative coalition leader, 69; foreign policy, 92, 94
Business Roundtable, 69

campaign spending, 4, 10; effect of
donations, 64; importance of, 24;
reforms, 114

Cantwell, Maria, 33

capitalism, 107; antagonism toward, 88;
criticism of, 65; failures of, 4–5, 40;
government limitation of, 6, 48;
imperialism as stage of, 88; logic of,
40; spread of, 90, 95; undemocratic
nature of, 41–42

Carter, Jimmy, 94

caucuses, 22

centralized planning, 6, 40; authoritarian tendencies in, 42; failures, 9, 41–
43, 46, 62, 87

centrists, 3

change, 14; catalysts for, 14, 105; causes
of, 87; by dominant parties, 18; lib-
eral-progressive, 11; movement for,
49; social (*see* social change); speed
of, 25

Chavez, Cesar, 52, 124; as leader, 73–
74, 77

Cheney, Richard, 54

China, 41, 87; defense of, 86

Christian Coalition, 28

Christian fundamentalists, 55

CIO (Congress of Industrial Organizations), 89–90

Citizen's Party (1980), 3

civil disobedience, 50

Civil Rights Act (1964), 56

civil rights movement, 6–7, 13, 14;
black–white rift, 57; Democratic
Party change and, 22–24, 34; group
framing by, 67; historically, 21; leaders, 27; strategic nonviolence in, 51;
tactics of, 53; violence against,
52–53; violence by, 56–57

class conflict, 21, 23, 50; social change
and, 65

classes, 63; American preferences and,

66; capitalist, 64; interests of, 21;
ownership, 6; problem-framing in
terms of, 65; ruling, 72

Clinton, Bill, 23, 31, 74; foreign policy
and, 94; media stance on, 102

coalitions, 2, 18; corporate-conservative
(*see* corporate-conservative coalition); within Democratic Party,
23–24; egalitarian, 68–69; farm
workers, 73; in global justice movement, 60; of groups/organizations,
78, 81; left-liberal-labor, 2–3, 89; liberal, 24; liberal-labor (*see* liberal-
labor coalition); umbrella, 82–83;
parties as, 2; pressures to create, 1;
value-based, 66; white–black, 106

Commission on Presidential Debates,
100

communism and communists, 2; failures of, 42; human rights and, 92;
support for, 86–96, 107

Communist Party, 88–90, 105

community, 97–98

competition, 46, 47, 48

compromise, 25, 27, 79

conflict: bases of, 91, 93; increasing,
25–26

confrontation, 106

Congress of Industrial Organizations
(CIO), 89–90

conservatives, 10–11, 113; Democratic
Party control by, 21–23; market theory and, 45; Republican Party membership, 35

constitutionalism, 78

consultant's role, 8

conventions, 4–5, 20

conversion, 67

cooperation, 47, 71

corporate-conservative coalition, 6, 9;
conditions created by, 28; Democrats within, 69; leadership of, 64;

opponents of, 9–10, 30; as opposition, 68, 69–70, 107; winning political power from, 45

corporations: advocacy statements by, 101; criticism of, 6; domination by, 122 (*see also* corporate-conservative coalition); executives, 64, 69; failures of, 3; market intervention tools, 44; multinational, 40, 95; power of, 13; rights of, 45; union organization against, 80

corruption, 42

Corzine, Jon, 5, 70

criminal justice system, 57

cults, 76

decentralization, 8, 43–44; market system as, 48; of movement structure, 81–82

DeLacy, Hugh, 112

democracy, 72; commitment to, 51; expansion methods, 7; lack of, 41; planning leading to, 87, 88; right to participate in, 92–93; support of, 93, 96; undemocratic regimes, 86–96

Democratic Leadership Council, 23, 28, 69

Democratic National Convention, egalitarians' role in, 30

Democratic Party: activists and, 32–33; change from civil rights movement, 22–24, 54; coalitions within, 23–24; criticism of, 31–32; egalitarian clubs in, 5, 7, 28, 79; egalitarians in, 3–4, 7, 26, 28; historical control of, 20–22, 34; left-liberal-labor coalition in, 2–3, 89; machine Democrats, 21, 22, 25, 54, 113; message/image of, 24–25, 35; Nader's campaign against, 77; social identities within, 30; supporters' interests, 33–34, 36; takeover areas, 29; takeover of, 19, 49, 62;

unions and, 80; votes for, 24, 95; White House control by, 5–6; working within, 78

Democratic Party transformation, 20, 22, 28–29; confrontation in, 106; group framing for, 68; out-group/ opposition identification, 68–70; strategies, 28–31; from within, 74–75

Democratic Socialists of America, 115

Democratic Workers Party, 75–76, 77

demonization, 54, 65, 68

dictatorships, 51

diplomats, 27

direct-action tactics, 7

districts, geographical, 1

Dixon, Marlene, 75–76

domination, 71–72; egotism in, 73, 74–75; by leaders, 71, 72–73; by nation-states, 85; organizations and, 72

dominators, 10, 110; capitalists as, 64–65; excluding, 78; leaders as, 71; neutralizing, 71–72; use of violence, 51

Dyson, Freeman, 97

earned income tax credit, 47, 70

economic aid, 96

economic concentration, 63–65

economic system: alternative visions/ plans for, 39–41, 45; authoritarianism in, 87; capitalists' domination of, 64; centrally planned (*see* centralized planning); change through, 87; changing, 19; democracy as result of planning in, 87–88; disasters in, 36–37; global, 95–96; nonmarket solutions, 45–46; socialist, 40

education, 45

egalitarian Democratic clubs, 5, 7, 28; in organizational network, 79

egalitarian-domination dimension,
10–12
egalitarian movement, 13–15, 105;
attraction of, 99, 101, 105; conflict
within, 86; divisiveness potential,
82–83; domination by leaders,
72–73; faith-based groups in, 97; foreign policy stance (*see* foreign policy); Iron Law of Oligarchy and, 76;
methods, 15; opposition to, 99,
106–7; organizational network for,
78–80; origins of, 66; principles, 39;
rationale underlying, 15; religious
stance (*see* religion); rules for, 78–
80, 81; single-issue campaigns, 106;
spokesperson accountability, 77–78;
strategic nonviolence and (*see* strategic nonviolence); use of opportunity,
108
egalitarians, 1, 10, 11; conflict with liberals, 2, 25, 35–36, 78; criticism of,
12; group defined as, 12–13, 79; history, 12; as in-group, 68–69; isolation
from everyday people, 86; issues for,
28, 37; leaders, 8, 11; moral sensibili-
ties of, 25; past successes, 13, 22;
political power needed, 45; progress
under moderate governments, 26;
reinforcement of liberals, 27; support of Democrats, 30; third-party
voting by, 2; transformation of Democratic Party by (*see* Democratic
Party; Democratic Party transformation); wealthy as, 69–70
elected officials, roles of, 26–27
Electoral College, 112
electoral systems, 1; creating egalitarian
role in, 37; monitoring for fairness,
93; rules of, 17; in United States, 18–
19. *See also* politics
elites, 6, 11
elitism within egalitarianism, 36, 71,
106

enemies. *See* opposition
energy policy, 44
Engels, Friedrich, 40
environmental protection, 13, 62; through
market-based planning, 44
equality, 2; balance with efficiency, 43;
balance with freedom, 43; gender,
13, 86, 98; income, 47–48; increasing, 8, 12, 62; means to achieve, 91;
organizational, 11–12; racial/ethnic,
11, 13; social, 4; support for, 66, 91
ethnic groups, party representation of,
2
ethnocentrism, 91
experts, 9, 64, 100

failures, 12
fairness, increasing, 2, 8
false consciousness, 130
Farrakhan, Louis, 74
feminism, 11
feminist movement, 81–82
foreign policy, 85–96; differentiated
stance toward, 91–92; economic,
95–96; egalitarian values in, 96; mistakes, 9; noninterventionist stance,
86–87; Soviet Union's effect on, 88–
90, 96; U.S. intervention, 91, 94, 96
forgiveness, 67
freedom, 92; commitment to, 51; personal, 12
freedom rides, 54
free market, 6, 43
free trade, 95

gains, defending, 27, 106
gay and lesbian movement, 13, 54–56
Gingrich, Newt, 54
globalization, 59, 91
global justice movement, 59–62; decentralized structure of, 82; Marxists in,
91, 127

Goldwater, Barry, 20
Gorbachev, Mikhail, 14
Gore, Albert, Jr., 1, 4, 5, 19; criticism of, 33, 69, 76–77; Jackson and, 31, 74; as moderate, 23
government: appointments within, 5; "big government," 32; capitalists' domination of, 64; domination by, 48; movement support by, 80; non-market solutions involving, 45; ownership power, 43; pathways into, 3, 28; planning by, 6, 48; policymaking by, 9
governmental agencies, 48
government-owned enterprises, 46, 48, 49
government purchases, 6, 43, 48
government spending: for African Americans, 56; party interests in, 22; social services, 46
Great Depression, 14
Green Party, 6, 31, 36

health care, 5, 46; insurance for, 47
hierarchy, 10, 110; development of, 79; imperialism as, 85; invisible, 82
highways, 45
homophobia, 55, 92
homosexual rights, 13
human rights, 86, 91–93; to nation-state, 93, 96; of political minorities, 93; religious infringement on, 98
hypocrisy, 55, 93

identity: class, 66; collective, 28–29, 30, 66, 69; need for, 67; political, 50, 51, 68; shared, 51; social, 25, 66, 68–69, 78, 79
imperialism, 85, 88, 90; economic, 93, 95–96
income leveling, 47
income tax, 48

in-groups, 65, 67; joining, 67–68; religious, 97
instant runoff voting, 19
insurance industry, 46
interest groups, 80
interests: of classes, 21, 66; divergent, 10
internationalism, 85–86, 96
International Monetary Fund, 96
International Socialist Organization, 127
Iron Law of Oligarchy, 72–73, 76, 79, 83
Israeli–Palestinian conflict, 93, 94

Jackson, Jesse, 30, 31; as leader, 74–75, 77
Johnson, Lyndon B., 56
journalism. See media
judicial appointees, 32

Kefauver, Estes, 20, 113
King, Martin Luther, Jr., 26, 57
Koppel, Ted, 35

labor: exploitation of, 41, 43, 47, 88; low-wage, 47; organized, 115. See also unions; workers
laws, breaking, 26
lawyers, 9
leadership and leaders: accountability of, 12, 71–83; controls on, 126; domination by, 11, 33, 72, 111; elected, 78; in media, 101; moral authority of, 74; organizations of, 79; power maintenance by, 75; power struggles within, 42; replaceability of, 12; use of violence, 51
left: in antiwar movements, 90; congressional representatives from, 18, 112; electoral setback for, 36; history of, 86–91, 105; Marxist influences on,

8–9; social movements' story, 63; third party of, 1–2; view of media, 100

Lenin, Vladimir, 87, 88

Lewis, John, 27

liberal-conservative dimension, 10–11

liberal-labor coalition, 9–10, 12, 79–80; Democratic Party and, 21

liberals, 6, 24, 49; conflict with egalitarians, 2, 25, 35–36, 78; Democrats, 21; distinction from activists, 26; reinforcement by egalitarians, 27

libertarians, 45

Lieberman, Joseph, 69

litigation, 13

living-wage movement, 13, 80–81

lobbyists, 9, 64

London, Meyer, 112

Mafia, 20, 21

majority vote, 1–2, 19

Mandela, Nelson, 14

Marcantonio, Vito, 112

marches, 54

market-based planning, 6, 8, 70; class structure alteration by, 66; foreign economic policy and, 95–96; policy and program development, 48; support requirement, 78; tools for, 43–44

markets: free, 6, 43; government intervention in, 39–48; limits of, 13; Marxist view of, 41–42, 117; necessity of, 45

market system, 47, 48; critiques of, 46; egalitarian, 95; entities competing in, 46, 48; equality in, 43; failures of, 45–46; as government planning tool, 5, 43; restructuring, 43–44, 48, 62, 95, 106–7

Marshall Plan, 89

Marx, Karl, 40

Marxism, 8–9; criticism of utopian planning, 40; internationalism in, 87; SDS factions and, 58; in United States, 87–89; view of market, 41–42, 117

mass transit, 45

meaning, 97

media, 99–104, 106; bypassing, 100; exposure, 100; independence of, 103; issue framing and importance, 100, 101–2; negative attention from, 60; negative news, 102; opinion range in, 100–101; ownership and control of, 100–101; use of, 13, 103, 104

message, strength of, 4

Middle Eastern countries, 93

moral credibility, 50

morale, 42

moral exemplars, 26, 102

Moral Majority, 28

moral sense, 25

Nader, Ralph, 19, 99–100; campaign explanation by, 31–37; campaign failures, 37, 76–77; campaign's effect, 36, 77, 99; debate participation, 100, 129; hypothetical 2000 campaign, 1–7; interest protection by, 34, 36; as leader, 76–77

name recognition, 4

nationalism, 93

National Labor Relations Act (1935), 21, 26

National Organization for Women (NOW), 81–82

nation-state, right to, 93, 96

negotiators, 27

networks: friendship, 4; nationwide, 82–83; of organizations, 78–80; policy-planning, 9

New Deal, 14, 26, 46

New Right, 3
newspapers, 99
Nixon, Richard M., 32
noninterventionism, 86, 90, 91, 96
nonviolence, strategic. *See* strategic
  nonviolence
nonvoters, 35, 116
North, nominations in, 3
NOW (National Organization for
  Women), 81–82

O'Connell, Jerry, 112
oligarchy. *See* Iron Law of Oligarchy
opportunity, 14, 34, 108
opposition: antagonism toward, 67;
  identifying, 6–7, 63–70; nonmem-
  bers, 68
out-groups, 65, 67, 104, 107
outing, 54–55

pacifists, 2
Palestinians, 93, 94
parliamentary systems, 2, 17; coalitions
  in, 18; in United States, 19
Peace and Freedom Party (1968), 3
Perot, H. Ross, 33, 35
pessimism, 14
planning: centralized (*see* centralized
  planning); information for, 42, 43;
  market-based (*see* market-based
  planning)
police, 52, 53, 119–20
policy, principle-based, 39
political experience, 31
political majority, difficulty of assembling, 10
political parties: centrist, 18; as extension of government, 3; increasing
  number of, 19; influencing from
  within, 5; membership of, 3; as pathway to government, 28; similarity of,
  34; takeover of, 5

politicians, 26–27; creating, 79; denigra-
  tion of, 28, 36
politics: class in, 65–66; local-level, 81;
  new ideas in, 35; participation in, 78,
  79; success in, 95
pollution, 5, 42, 44
Populist Party, 27
poverty, 5
power, 10; challenges to, 106; of corporations, 13, 107; decision-making, 73;
  of leaders, 11; masking, 126; of
  media, 99; of nation-states, 91; political, 65; of southern rich, 23
power context, 110
power structures, 40, 71; ideology in,
  107; informal, 82; inverted, 71, 72,
  83; in United States, 9
presidency, 18, 112; abolishing, 19
press, freedom of, 103
primaries, 3, 20; egalitarians in, 28–29;
  insurgents in, 3, 30–31; turnout for,
  29
productivity, 43
profit, 41, 101, 117
Progressive Party (1948), 2–3, 89
progressives, 6, 26
proletariat, 63
property destruction. *See* strategic nonviolence
proportional representation, 17, 18–19
public opinion, liberalization of, 58

racism and racists, 67, 92, 106
radicals, 6, 11
Rainbow Coalition, 74
rallies, 4
Randolph, A. Philip, 89
redemption, 67
reform, 34
reformers, 11, 103
regulation, 6, 43, 48
religion, 51, 96–98; as conflict basis, 93;

conflicts with, 8, 97, 107; criticism of, 98; power alignment, 97
religious tolerance, 92, 98
Republican Party: backlash against, 34; coalition-forming within, 13–14; corporate-conservative coalition in, 9; corporate financing of, 2; egalitarian view of, 32; foreign policy, 94–95; gay members, 54–55; as opposition, 34, 68, 107; organizations within, 28; power history, 23; as rich person's party, 21, 23; third parties as aid to, 35
research, 13
responses, forcing, 39
revolution, 58, 88
Rice, Condoleezza, 92
right: economic issues, 35; social movements' story, 63; third party of, 1–2; unity of, 32
rights: of corporations, 45; to employment, 47; equal (see equality); human (see human rights); preserving, 14
Rockefeller, John D., Jr., 35
Roosevelt, Franklin D., 89, 102
routine, 49–50, 53; commitment to everyday lives, 108, 130; disruption of, 53, 54, 62

Sanders, Bernie, 112
sanitation, public, 45
SDS (Students for a Democratic Society), 58–59, 90, 105
segregation, 56
SEIU (Service Employees International Union), 81
self-determination, 86, 91, 93, 96
seniority, congressional, 22, 23
Service Employees International Union (SEIU), 81
sexism, 92

sexual orientation. See gay and lesbian movement
Sinclair, Upton, 3
single-member district plurality system, 1–2, 17, 18, 112; civil rights movement changes to, 34–35
sit-ins, 54
SNCC (Student Nonviolent Coordinating Committee), 56, 105
social change, 6; class framing and, 65–66; egalitarians' role in, 105; electoral dimension of, 27; group framing strategies, 67–70; inclusiveness strategies, 65–67; large-scale, 8; methods for, 53; opponent identification, 63–70; opposition to, 68; organizations for, 63; single-issue campaigns, 106; worse-the-better theory, 25–26, 32–33
Social Democratic Party (Germany), 73
social disruption, 49–50, 53, 62
socialism: centralized planning and, 6; failures, 6, 39, 40–41; market, 41–42, 43, 117; opposition to, 90; party formation, 87
socialists, 2, 6, 107; in Congress, 18
social movement organizations, 7, 27; effectiveness of, 26; formal structure lack, 126; group framing and, 67; members as egalitarian in-group, 68–69; role of, 48
social movements, need for, 49
Social Security, 35
social stratification, 10, 63–64
Soros, George, 69–70
South: Democratic Party history in, 21–22; industrialization of, 23; nominations in, 3; power of, 24; white primaries in, 20, 113
South Africa, 14, 18, 93
Soviet Union, 14, 41; American Communists and, 88–89; defense of, 86;

foreign policy influence, 88–90, 96;
    reasons for failure of, 42–43, 87
speech, freedom of, 10, 114
Stalin, Joseph, 87
states' rights, 18–19
status groups, 66
stereotypes, 54
Stevenson, Adlai, 20
strategic nonviolence, 7, 27, 50–62;
    adherence lapses, 56–62; advocat-
    ing, 92; commitment to, 36, 62, 79,
    82; difficulty of, 107; environment
    for use, 53; goals of, 62; media use
    strategies, 99; methods, 13, 49, 50,
    53–56; requirements for, 50–51
strategy, criticism of, 13
strikes, 9, 50
Student Nonviolent Coordinating Com-
    mittee (SNCC), 56, 105
Students for a Democratic Society
    (SDS), 58–59, 90, 105
subsidies, 6, 43, 48; earned income tax
    credit, 47; job, 44
support programs, 47–48

taxes, 6, 43, 48; corporate-conservative
    coalition ideology re, 46; earned
    income tax credit, 47, 70; income,
    48; subsidy financing through, 44
television, 99
Tennessee Valley Authority, 46
terminology, 12–13
terrorism, 96
third parties, 1, 17; building support for,
    25–26; as choice, 31; as Democratic
    spoilers, 103, 107; eschewing, 81, 82;
    futility of, 8, 62, 106; impact of, 3,
    35; media and, 103–4; odds against,
    7–8, 20; preference for, 25; struc-
    tural constraints on, 21, 62; time
    needed to build, 33–34; in United
    States, 18; virtues of, 33, 35

Trotsky, Leon, 87
Truman, Harry, 102
two-party system. See single-member
    district plurality system

unions, 9; 1930s movement, 34; coali-
    tions and, 24; communist organizing
    of, 88–89; creation of, 13; in global
    justice movement, 60; integration of,
    56; in organizational network,
    79–80; revival of, 14; United Farm
    Workers, 73–74; working-class mem-
    bers, 65–66. See also labor; workers
United Farm Workers, 73–74
United Nations, 93–94, 96
U.S. Chamber of Commerce, 69
us-versus-them issue, 67–70, 79
utopian movements, 39–40

value, surplus, 41, 117
values, 12, 14, 50; egalitarian, 91–92,
    96, 107; in market system, 46; plural-
    istic, 98; universal, 96
Vietnam War, 58–59, 90–91
violence, 12; by civil rights activists,
    56–57; counterproductive, 52,
    105–6; distancing from perpetrators,
    62; by dominant class, 50, 52; forcing
    protection against, 54; by govern-
    ment, 21, 50, 52; justifications for,
    51–52; marginalizing proponents of,
    7, 61; media blamed for, 99–100;
    media focus on, 58, 60, 102, 104;
    negative effects of, 57–62, 119–20;
    opposition to, 8; refraining from, 50–
    52, 107; retaliation for, 50, 52
vote: minimum, 17–18; for party, 24;
    predictors of, 116
voter turnout, 18
Voting Rights Act (1965), 34, 56

wage relationship, 41–42, 46
Wallace, Henry, 2, 36, 89, 105

wealth distribution, 63–64
Williams, Pete, 55
women, 81–82
women's suffrage, 13
workers, 41–42; protection of, 47, 62;
    union representation of, 80. *See also*
    labor; unions

Workers World Party, 127
working class, 65, 68
World Bank, 96
World Trade Organization (WTO), 59,
    95, 96. *See also* global justice move-
    ment
worse-the-better theory, 25–26, 32–33

ABOUT THE AUTHOR

G. William Domhoff is research professor at the University of California, Santa Cruz, where he teaches courses on power, politics, and social change. He is a graduate of Duke University, Kent State University, and the University of Miami. Four of his earlier books are on the list of top-50 best-sellers in sociology since World War II: *Who rules America?* (1967), *The higher circles* (1970), *The powers that be* (1979), and *Who rules America now?* (1983). His recent books include *State autonomy or class dominance?* (1996) and *Who rules America?* 4th ed. (2002).